The Blizzard of 1888

The Blizzard of 1888

Tracee de Hahn

CHELSEA HOUSE PUBLISHERS
Philadelphia

CHELSEA HOUSE PUBLISHERS

Production Manager Pamela Loos
Art Director Sara Davis
Director of Photography Judy L. Hasday
Managing Editor James D. Gallagher
Senior Production Editor J. Christopher Higgins

Staff for THE BLIZZARD OF 1888

Senior Editor John Ziff
Editorial Assistant Rob Quinn
Associate Art Director/Designer Takeshi Takahashi
Picture Researcher Sandy Jones
Cover Designer Emiliano Begnardi

First Printing

1 3 5 7 9 8 6 4 2

The Chelsea House World Wide Web address is
http://www.chelseahouse.com

Library of Congress Cataloging-in-Publication Data

De Hahn, Tracee.
The blizzard of 1888 / Tracee de Hahn.
  p. cm. — (Great disasters: reforms and ramifications)
Includes bibliographical references and index.

ISBN 0-7910-5787-9

1. New York (N.Y.)—History—1865-1898—Juvenile
literature. 2. Blizzards—New York (State)—New York—
History—19th century—Juvenile literature. 3. Northeastern
States—History—19th century—Juvenile literature. 4.
Blizzards—Northeastern States—History—19th century—
Juvenile literature. [1. Blizzards—New York (State)—New
York. 2. Blizzards—Northeastern States. 3. New York
(N.Y.)—History—1865-1898.] I. Title. II. Great disasters:
reforms and ramifications.

F128.47.D4 2000
974.7'1041—dc21

00-043081

Contents

GREAT DISASTERS
REFORMS and RAMIFICATIONS

THE *APOLLO 1* AND
CHALLENGER DISASTERS

THE BLIZZARD OF 1888

THE BOMBING OF HIROSHIMA

THE *EXXON VALDEZ*

THE GREAT CHICAGO FIRE

THE *HINDENBURG*

THE HOLOCAUST

THE INFLUENZA PANDEMIC OF 1918

THE JOHNSTOWN FLOOD

PEARL HARBOR

THE SAN FRANCISCO EARTHQUAKE
OF 1906

THE STOCK MARKET CRASH OF 1929

TERRORISM

THREE MILE ISLAND

THE *TITANIC*

THE TRIANGLE SHIRTWAIST COMPANY
FIRE OF 1911

Jill McCaffrey
National Chairman
Armed Forces Emergency Services
American Red Cross

Introduction

Disasters have always been a source of fascination and awe. Tales of a great flood that nearly wipes out all life are among humanity's oldest recorded stories, dating at least from the second millennium B.C., and they appear in cultures from the Middle East to the Arctic Circle to the southernmost tip of South America and the islands of Polynesia. Typically gods are at the center of these ancient disaster tales—which is perhaps not too surprising, given the fact that the tales originated during a time when human beings were at the mercy of natural forces they did not understand.

To a great extent, we still are at the mercy of nature, as anyone who reads the newspapers or watches nightly news broadcasts can attest.

Hurricanes, earthquakes, tornados, wildfires, and floods continue to exact a heavy toll in suffering and death, despite our considerable knowledge of the workings of the physical world. If science has offered only limited protection from the consequences of natural disasters, it has in no way diminished our fascination with them. Perhaps that's because the scale and power of natural disasters force us as individuals to confront our relatively insignificant place in the physical world and remind us of the fragility and transience of our lives. Perhaps it's because we can imagine ourselves in the midst of dire circumstances and wonder how we would respond. Perhaps it's because disasters seem to bring out the best and worst instincts of humanity: altruism and selfishness, courage and cowardice, generosity and greed.

As one of the national chairmen of the American Red Cross, a humanitarian organization that provides relief for victims of disasters, I have had the privilege of seeing some of humanity's best instincts. I have witnessed communities pulling together in the face of trauma; I have seen thousands of people answer the call to help total strangers in their time of need.

Of course, helping victims after a tragedy is not the only way, or even the best way, to deal with disaster. In many cases planning and preparation can minimize damage and loss of life—or even avoid a disaster entirely. For, as history repeatedly shows, many disasters are caused not by nature but by human folly, shortsightedness, and unethical conduct. For example, when a land developer wanted to create a lake for his exclusive resort club in Pennsylvania's Allegheny Mountains in 1880, he ignored expert warnings and cut corners in reconstructing an earthen dam. On May 31, 1889, the dam gave way, unleashing 20 million tons of water on the towns below. The Johnstown Flood, the deadliest in American history, claimed more than 2,200 lives. Greed and negligence would figure prominently in the Triangle Shirtwaist Company fire in 1911. Deplorable conditions in the garment sweatshop, along with a failure to give any thought to the safety of workers, led to the tragic deaths of 146 persons. Technology outstripped wisdom only a year later, when the designers of the luxury liner *Titanic* smugly declared their state-of-the-art ship "unsinkable," seeing no need to provide lifeboat capacity for everyone onboard. On the night of April 14, 1912, more than 1,500 passengers and crew paid for this hubris with their lives after the ship collided with an iceberg and sank. But human catastrophes aren't always the unforeseen consequences of carelessness or folly. In the 1940s the leaders of Nazi Germany purposefully and systematically set out to exterminate all Jews, along with Gypsies, homosexuals, the mentally ill, and other so-called undesirables. More recently terrorists have targeted random members of society, blowing up airplanes and buildings in an effort to advance their political agendas.

The books in the GREAT DISASTERS: REFORMS AND RAMIFICATIONS series examine these and other famous disasters, natural and human made. They explain the causes of the disasters, describe in detail how events unfolded, and paint vivid portraits of the people caught up in dangerous circumstances. But these books are more than just accounts of what happened to whom and why. For they place the disasters in historical perspective, showing how people's attitudes and actions changed and detailing the steps society took in the wake of each calamity. And in the end, the most important lesson we can learn from any disaster—as well as the most fitting tribute to those who suffered and died—is how to avoid a repeat in the future.

A Glimpse of Spring, a Return to Winter

High winds drive the snow in the early hours of the Blizzard of '88. Before the three-day storm had ended, snowfall that reached 50 inches in some areas would paralyze the northeastern United States.

When U.S. Army sergeant Francis Long arrived at work on a mild Saturday in March, he could not have predicted that within 24 hours he would be faced with a death-defying task made necessary by one of the worst winter storms the Northeast had ever seen. Sergeant Long had spent years in the unsettled West and the frozen Arctic. He hardly expected his desk job at the New York City branch of the U.S. Signal Service to be dangerous.

But the winter storm that began on Sunday, March 11, 1888, and tore across the northeastern United States changed a lot of people's minds about the safety of the city. That storm, which gave Sergeant Long a taste of the adventure he thought he had long left behind, has remained so prominent a fixture in weather folklore that it is simply known as the

Blizzard of '88. Although it lasted only three days, from March 11 to March 13, the storm left a legacy of record low temperatures, heavy snow, and nearly 400 people dead. The storm's severity was emphasized by its arrival on the heels of a fine weekend barely a week and a half before the vernal equinox, which marks the first official day of spring.

The Blizzard of '88 is also remembered for its social impact. At a time of great confidence in the progress of technology, the storm caused people to question their faith in the technologically advanced modern city. The storm not only awed people with its force, but it was directly responsible for important changes that took place in American cities at the turn of the century.

In the United States the last decades of the 1800s have been called the Age of Confidence. It is easy to understand why. The generation of Americans born after the end of the Civil War in 1865 had known peace and increasing prosperity at home. While those who yearned for wide-open spaces could still find plenty of land in the West, those who wanted an alternative to frontier (or even rural) living gravitated toward the expanding cities.

The rapid growth of American cities in the late 1800s was part of a much larger trend termed the industrial age or the industrial revolution. The product of advances in science and technology, the industrial revolution—which had originated in England—brought profound changes to society. The advent of steam-powered machines allowed factories to produce large quantities of goods much faster than had been possible with the hand-production methods formerly used. This not only generated vast wealth for the industrialists who owned the factories, but also created a need for large numbers of factory workers. Though the work was difficult, the hours long, the pay generally low, and the conditions often danger-

ous, factory jobs were desirable because they provided a regular paycheck, freeing people from the unpredictability of farming. Factory work was especially appealing to new immigrants who had no land to farm and thus few options for earning a living.

As the industrial revolution took hold, the proportion of people working on farms declined, whereas the proportion working in factories rose. Because factories required a large labor supply, they were located in cities. This, in turn, fueled the further growth of the cities, as people in search of work moved there and became part of the working (or laboring) class.

By the winter of 1888 the eastern seaboard communities of the United States—particularly Boston, New York City, Philadelphia, and Washington, D.C.—felt the

A New York City street scene, late 1800s. Fueled by immigration from abroad and the influx of residents from the countryside, America's cities experienced explosive growth in the latter part of the 19th century. The Blizzard of '88 would make it abundantly clear that the infrastructure of the city hadn't kept pace with the needs of so many inhabitants.

Like these people enjoying a carriage ride through New York City's Central Park, Americans went outdoors in droves to take advantage of the beautiful spring weekend that preceded the blizzard. When they settled into their beds on Sunday night, March 11, few could have imagined that the next days would bring the winter storm of the century.

changes brought about by the industrial age. These cities were larger than ever before, as Americans from the countryside joined a flood of immigrants from Ireland, Italy, Russia, Poland, and Germany in search of a better way of life in the metropolises of the United States. For example, the population of New York City's island center, Manhattan, had grown an astonishing 26 percent in the 1880s alone. Immigrants accounted for much of the population growth: the 1890 New York census showed that four out of five residents had been born outside the United States.

As the laboring class moved to the city, wealthy citizens looked out across America and saw increased production in the factories, an endless supply of workers, and opportunities for increased affluence. All in all, America was a land of bustling opportunity, and no place reflected this more than New York City.

Sergeant Long was among the growing masses of optimistic city dwellers. And whatever their address, job description, or native language, the inhabitants of the East Coast shared one thing with him the afternoon of Saturday, March 10, 1888: they were all enjoying a beautiful spring day. No one would have predicted that in less than 24 hours the winter storm of the century would be upon them, affecting one-fourth of the nation's population and covering 10 states, 12 major cities, and hundreds of towns. On the March weekend before the storm, trees were budding in New York City's Central Park, farmers were planting potatoes on Long Island, and spring was in the air. In New Haven, Connecticut, young men attending Yale University spent the day on the riverbank rowing and picnicking, while wealthy city dwellers took the train to their country mansions. Even scattered showers and slightly lower temperatures on Sunday didn't dampen spirits along the coast. After the mildest winter in 17 years, residents and weather forecasters alike decided that winter deserved its last gasp before spring officially arrived.

In New York City newly arrived immigrants often spent the day of rest enjoying the cafés, clubs, and music halls that city law had recently allowed open on Sunday. It was the one day of the week when a member of the laboring class had time to see friends, sip a glass of wine or beer, and relax. Recent arrivals from the countryside often used their free day to visit relatives, traveling miles using the elevated railroad or horsecar. As a result, these city laborers were the first to realize that Sunday night was not ending the way the weekend had begun.

In Brooklyn two German-Americans walking their young ladies home after an evening of dancing found the gutters overflowing in a torrential rain. As they chivalrously offered to carry their companions—hoping to save their long dresses and high-heeled boots from a thorough soaking—the situation quickly turned from the hilarious end of a fun evening to a treacherous journey: the rain had turned to sleet and the sidewalks were coated with ice. These young men would have been astonished if they had happened upon a newsboy selling the early-morning edition of the New York newspaper the *Herald*. At midnight on Sunday the weather forecast for Monday read: "In this city and suburban districts today colder, partly cloudy to fair weather and brisk to fresh westerly to northwesterly winds will probably prevail followed by clear conditions."

In New York City during the hours between midnight on Sunday, March 11, and noon on Monday, March 12, rain turned to sleet, the temperature dropped from 33°F to 14°F, and the wind began gusting in blasts up to 84 miles per hour (mph). So why was the forecast still so optimistic? Sergeant Long and the other men responsible for the weather indicators—as the weather forecast was then called—would be among the first to realize the limits of what was considered advanced technology.

The men worked for the U.S. Signal Service. Established by Congress in 1870 by order of President Ulysses S. Grant, the United States Signal Service (parent of the present-day National Weather Service) operated telegraph stations from which meteorological reports could be dispatched across the country. This army weather service was created after the storms of 1868 and 1869 sank or damaged 3,000 ships and caused the loss of 530 lives on the Great Lakes.

One of the Signal Service stations was in New York City, at that metropolis's highest site: the tower of the brand-new Equitable Assurance Building. At a then remarkable seven stories, the tower rose 150 feet above the city, a perfect location for monitoring the weather. Visitors, drawn by an industrial-age fascination with advances in science and technology, could reach the station using the first hydraulic elevators in the world and, in the words of one guidebook, "look down from this dizzying height upon the marvelous stretch of scenery taking in the Narrows, Staten Island, the North and East River, and the major portions of New York and Brooklyn." Out-of-town visitors were encouraged to include the station in their tour of New York and could walk out on the roof to examine the instruments that measured humidity, rain, wind, and temperature. As long as they did not interfere with the operation of the station, visitors were also encouraged to observe the noncommissioned officers and enlisted men in the Army Signal Corps who manned the station. And while most visitors came to marvel at the technology of the industrial age, some may have made the journey to the weather station tower specifically to have Sergeant Francis Long pointed out to them.

At seven stories, the Equitable Assurance Building was New York City's tallest structure and an ideal location for a U.S. Signal Service weather station.

Sergeant Long had enjoyed a colorful career in the U.S. Army and had joined the Army Signal Service when his former superior became commander. On Saturday, March 10, despite his knowledge of weather patterns and access to a network of equipment and reports, Sergeant

Signal Service employees at work in a weather station's "fact room," where indicators, or forecasts, were produced.

Long was certainly among those who would not have believed danger was so near at hand.

That is not to say that Signal Service personnel were unaware of bad weather in the area. Three times a day—at 7 A.M., 3 P.M., and 10 P.M.—the 170 regular government weather stations sent telegraphed reports to headquarters in Washington, D.C. These reports included uncorrected readings of barometric pressure, dry and wet temperature, dew point temperature, relative humidity, wind velocity and direction, cloudiness, precipitation, current weather, and totals and averages for a variety of meteorological quantities. Contributing to this information were approximately 2,000 volunteers across the country, working under the guidance of the Smithsonian Institution and the Surgeon General's office. After analyzing the data, the Washington station would send a report to each outlying station on the weather that would affect its region.

AN AMERICAN LEGEND: SERGEANT FRANCIS LONG

Sergeant Francis Long emigrated from Germany as a teenager in the 1860s. A big, red-haired, fun-loving man, he was known as a good storyteller. After arriving in the United States he joined the Army of the West, seeking work and adventure, and finding it with 10 years of Indian fighting.

On June 26, 1876, his company was ordered toward the Little Bighorn River, where General George Armstrong Custer's 7th Cavalry was confronting the Sioux Indians and their allies. Fortunately for Long, his company was still 20 miles away when General Custer's famous "Last Stand" resulted in the death of 14 officers and 250 enlisted men. Long later told friends that he was the first to reach the battlefield the next day, finding Custer and some of the other officers. Although no one ever verified his claim, it was a great story and became part of his legend.

Continuing his quest for adventure, Sergeant Long volunteered as cook for an 1881 Arctic expedition under the command of General Adolphus W. Greely. Mistakes on the part of the crew, coupled with bad luck, left the party stranded in the frozen Arctic. Months later, in 1882, a relief ship was unable to find Greely's party. In fact, it wasn't until June 1884 that the party was finally rescued. By this time Long was the only man who still had the strength to move. He was discovered several miles from the camp crawling on his hands and knees, half frozen and with a gun in his hand, searching for food for the others. Years of cold and hunger had taken a big toll: of the 25 original members of the expedition only 6, including Long, survived.

Newspapers had closely followed the story of the lost expedition, so Long returned to the United States a celebrity. He was given a good deal of credit for the survival of his five comrades. He had hunted and trapped in the bitter cold of the Arctic, bringing in a 400-pound bear just when the men had resorted to eating their leather belts. Now his friendly nature and love of storytelling came in handy. He toured, lecturing on his adventures, until he had enough money saved to marry and settle in Brooklyn. There his former boss and fellow survivor, General Greely, asked him to try his hand at a new, less adventurous job: reading weather charts and watching the weather.

On the Saturday before the storm, the New York City station was aware of weather disturbances to the west. Specifically, an enormous area of low pressure—called a trough—was coming east at 600 miles per day. It had dusted Kentucky and Tennessee with snow and sent temperatures near freezing in Georgia, with frost appearing on the ground as far south as Mississippi and Alabama. In addition, other low-pressure centers—potential creators of tornadoes—were near Green Bay, Wisconsin, and over St. Louis, Missouri. On Saturday a midday report from Washington, D.C., said that the southern low-pressure center had moved to the southeast, bringing heavy rain to Georgia and Florida, and that rain or snow was falling all the way north to Michigan.

Just before midnight on Saturday, the New York station prepared its indicator (forecast) for the next day based on information relayed by telegraph through the Washington station from all stations farther west. These stations reported that the low-pressure trough was now approaching the Appalachian Mountains, indicating that it would soon clear Kentucky and center on the Virginias. The low-pressure center in Wisconsin had phased out, and the southern one was heading out to sea near Cape Hatteras, North Carolina. Streams of very cold Canadian air were flowing into Newfoundland and the New England states, where they would be coming up against a stalled or very slow moving area of high pressure. Based on this information, the indicator read:

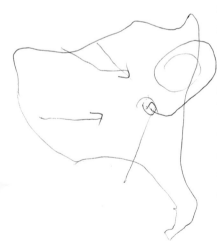

For Maine, New Hampshire, Vermont, Massachusetts, Rhode Island, Connecticut, eastern New York, eastern Pennsylvania, and New Jersey, fresh to brisk south-easterly winds, slightly warmer, fair weather, followed by rain.

For the District of Columbia, Maryland, Delaware, and Virginia, fresh to brisk southeasterly winds, slightly warmer, threatening weather and rain.

This indicator was sent to newspapers and private subscribers who paid to receive weather reports by telegram.

At midnight sharp on Saturday, the New York station closed to observe the Sabbath. The station would reopen at 5 P.M. Sunday, after having been left unmanned for 17 hours. In those 17 hours conditions along the coast would change dramatically, and within 24 hours the storm would arrive, bringing with it temperatures near 0°F, gusting winds, and several feet of snow. The unannounced blizzard would set records for sheer force and destructiveness of a storm, paralyze political and economic centers for hundreds of miles, and claim hundreds of unprepared lives. For the moment, however, the Washington, D.C., station was predicting "fair weather throughout the Atlantic States," and Sergeant Long and his fellow forecasters headed home under a moonless, starlit sky, confident in the Signal Service's claim of 82 percent accuracy.

Throughout the eastern seaboard, early risers on March 12 were greeted by a thick—and steadily rising—blanket of snow.

The Storm Hits

While a few late-night revelers might have realized that Sunday's rain was freezing, most of the population of the East Coast was fast asleep as the storm approached and blanketed city and countryside alike. The storm, which had been moving off the coast toward the Atlantic Ocean, shifted suddenly late Sunday evening. A counterclockwise rotation of winds around the trough picked up additional moisture as the system spun over the Atlantic Ocean. Instead of moving farther offshore, the storm started north. As it moved, the rotating winds accelerated, temperatures under the storm center dropped, and rain changed to snow.

Anyone tracking the storm today on a map could plot the swoop of its path: the center was focused near Atlanta, Georgia, at 7 A.M. on Sunday, March 11, bringing cool temperatures and rain. By three o'clock that afternoon it was near the Atlantic Ocean, over North Carolina's coast. As the center moved offshore around 10 P.M. on March 11, it began picking up speed and moisture. Although still centered offshore on Monday, March 12, the storm was large enough and strong enough to be felt in the coastal states as either rain or snow. Slowly these regions turned colder, and snow accumulated. From there the storm moved toward shore in a northwesterly direction, its center lodging over Block Island halfway between New York State's Long Island and the island of Nantucket, Massachusetts. Here it stayed for more than a day, wreaking havoc in the states of New York, Connecticut, Rhode Island, and Massachusetts. Finally, on March 13, the storm shifted, rolling first southwest, then southeast toward the ocean. By 7 A.M. on March 14, the storm was over the Atlantic Ocean, moving toward Europe, where it would hit Great Britain four days later. Altogether the storm traveled more than 1,200 miles between 7 A.M., March 11, and 7 A.M, March 14.

In the countryside, farmers, awake early to tend their livestock, were among the first to realize that in less than six hours rain had turned into freezing rain and then into heavy snow. Armed with experience, they and other country dwellers reacted to the winter storm as farmers had for centuries. Less dependent on modern conveniences such as indoor plumbing and electricity, they were able to retreat to a self-sufficient lifestyle. Most farming families were simply thankful the storm had hit while they were all safe in their beds: candles would provide light; firewood, always kept in supply by the door, would keep them warm; and the cellar was filled with food. While they might occasionally have sent and received a telegram, they certainly didn't depend on such conveniences for day-to-day living. Once a rope was stretched to the barn, allowing the animals to be reached

without losing one's way in the blowing snow, most farming families were prepared to wait out the storm, if not in total comfort, at least in relative safety.

It was a very different picture in the cities of the East Coast. Life had a different rhythm, and the city was only learning to accommodate the needs of millions of inhabitants. The storm would strain the new infrastructure of the city past the breaking point and illustrate the need to reexamine how technology was integrated into city life.

The first hint of a problem occurred before the late-night revelers had awakened to see the full force of the storm. The discovery of a blizzard was left to the bakers, newspaper delivery boys, and milkmen, who quickly realized they might not be able to go about their business as usual. When these early risers set out to work in the

At the height of the storm, pedestrians cross the Brooklyn Bridge. When the trains, horse-cars, and ferries they usually relied on stopped running, many commuters braved the elements to travel on foot to the factories, shops, and offices where they worked. Daily-wage workers in particular could ill afford to miss a day's pay.

The countryside abounded with lovely winter scenes such as this one. The beauty was deceptive, however: when the winds suddenly kicked up, the driving snow could reduce visibility to a few feet, and dozens of people froze to death on normally familiar terrain.

hours before dawn, approximately 10 inches of snow had already fallen in New York City. Worse than the snow was the layer of ice, often several inches thick, that made walking nearly impossible. As the early risers struggled against the elements, late or absent hot rolls, morning papers, and milk for the kids were the first indications for much of middle-class and wealthy New York that something was severely amiss.

Initially many people may have underestimated the power of the storm, particularly if they were unaccustomed to blizzards. And by Monday morning the weather across the eastern seaboard was not simply bad, it was severe enough to be called an official blizzard. In the United States a snowstorm must be accompanied by winds of at least 32 mph, low temperatures, and visibility reduced to less than 500 feet to be classified as a blizzard. If the temperature dips below 10°F and winds rise above 45 mph, the storm is classified as a severe blizzard. In any blizzard snowdrifts of 25 to 30 feet high are not considered unusual. These high drifts result when the wind blows snow against objects, such as fences or the sides of buildings, that trap the snow. The Blizzard of '88 quickly and easily slipped into the severe blizzard classification, with temperatures dropping to near zero in many places across the Northeast, winds gusting at 60 to 80 mph, and snowfall reaching 50 inches in some areas.

Remarkably similar winter conditions had hit the Great Plains in January of 1888, making headlines across the Northeast. That storm, which struck in the middle of the day, trapped children at school or, even worse, on the walk between school and home. During the blizzard on the Great Plains, newspapers in the East had been quick to point out the difficulties of living in the "wilderness." Many city dwellers were reminded why they had moved from the country and were thankful that the city protected them and their jobs from the unpredictability of nature. When the March blizzard struck the chain of coastal cities, many realized that the city in fact could *not* protect them from Mother Nature. Interestingly, newspapers then quickly focused on the "natural resilience" of the city dweller, using this theme throughout the news stories of the next four days.

While the size and force of the Blizzard of '88 continue to impress meteorologists more than 100 years later, the people who lived through it had more immediate concerns. In general the storm affected city dwellers much differently than it did citizens of the countryside, but even within the city there were vast differences in the storm's impact on people. Most differences were rooted in

(continued on p. 30)

Poster for Barnum and Bailey's circus, which played at Madison Square Garden during the blizzard.

THE SHOW MUST GO ON

The streets of Manhattan were especially busy on Saturday, March 10, Barnum and Bailey's Circus was in town, and thousands of spectators lined the route of the grand preopening parade. Eager faces even filled the upper-story windows of buildings along the route. At sunset the parade began with volunteer torchbearers who were each rewarded with a free ticket to the circus. After the torchbearers came a golden chariot filled with acrobats and bareback riders. The chariot was followed by a military band sporting uniforms of orange and gold. Behind the band came the animal cages. Pulled by horses, these elaborate cages carried lions, wolves, tigers, hyenas, bears, leopards, and monkeys. Then came a team of camels pulling a chariot whose passengers, to the delight of children and adults along the parade route, were Mother Goose and Cinderella. The final chariot, pulled by a team of elephants, was full of clowns.

P. T. Barnum himself was waiting to review the parade from a balcony at the Metropolitan Hotel on Broadway at Prince Street. As the parade neared the Metropolitan Hotel, Barnum, a lively old gentleman of 77, demonstrated the wit and quick thinking that had made his circus so successful. A fire broke out in the building across the street from his hotel, threatening to disrupt the parade route as people dispersed and fire wagons raced to the scene. Barnum cried, "Let the building go, I'll pay for it. I won't have this great multitude disappointed!" After he was sure a reporter had recorded his words—certain that the story would be great publicity for the circus—Barnum allowed police to reroute the parade to the next block, where he joined it riding in a cab.

During the night the storm struck, but the next day both P. T. Barnum and James Bailey arrived early at Madison Square Garden. No amount of snow or ice could keep them away, for they were determined that their circus, which they had humbly dubbed "the Greatest Show on Earth," would go on. Together the two men kept the afternoon and evening performances—86 acts in three rings—on schedule all week. For the few spectators who braved the weather to come to the circus, the sound of the band drowned out the noise of more than 100 shovels on the flat roof of Madison Square Garden. The shovelers were working to prevent the roof from collapsing under the weight of the snow and ice.

(continued from p. 27)

economic inequalities; the needs of the factory laborer differed greatly from those of the stockbroker, much less the wealthy industrialist. As always seems to be true, the laboring or working class was hardest hit by the storm.

William Brubaker was a milkman in New York City in 1888. Every morning at 2:30 he left his house with his horse and delivery wagon to travel from Manhattan to Jersey City, New Jersey, on the ferry. There he picked up fresh milk delivered by milk train from farms in the country. Well before dawn on the morning of March 12, Brubaker left his home as usual. It had been snowing for just over two hours, and he wore his thickest coat, gloves, and hat. Despite the mild winter, Brubaker was used to predawn cold and felt he was prepared. By the time he realized he was wrong, it was almost too late.

Normally the trip to Jersey City and back took two and a half hours, allowing Brubaker to begin delivery in the city around 5 A.M. On this day, however, the trip took five hours, twice as long as usual. Later, when he told friends that his horse had tried to turn back to the stable three times, Brubaker acknowledged that the "horse had more sense than I." The milkman was fortunate. Nearly exhausted, he stopped in a saloon to warm up with a glass of whiskey, and the bartender made him walk around for 10 minutes. As his hands, feet, and ears warmed up, they began to burn, a sure sign of frostbite. Brubaker decided to spend the rest of the storm at home—a wise decision that probably saved his life.

William Brubaker was one of the lucky members of the working class: he could decide to stay home from work and know that he would have a job when the storm was over. This was not true for most workers. At 7 A.M. on Monday, E. E. Handel boarded the elevated train at 84th Street in Manhattan, afraid that if he missed work he would lose his job as a salesman in a haberdashery, or men's clothing and accessories store. Almost immediately the journey turned perilous. As the train left the station, it accelerated past the legal limit of 12 mph in order to gain enough momentum to carry it uphill on the icy rails. "We went so fast out of the regular [station]," Handel later recounted, "that it soon became alarming. . . . I said we would have a collision and sure enough it came."

Blinded by blowing snow and fearful of causing a wreck, the conductor of the train in front of Handel's had not left the next station. Unfortunately the same blowing snow was blinding the conductor of Handel's train. According to a newspaper report, the conductor "put on all steam down the grade and approached the 76th Street station at a much greater speed than that usually attained by elevated trains." The result was disaster: the collision knocked the engine and the car that it struck into the air. They landed across the tracks, coming to rest leaning against the station.

E. E. Handel later remembered shouting, "Take it easy!" to his panicked fellow passengers. He also remembered that his advice had little effect. Passengers pressed forward in an effort to escape the derailed train, and in the crush of people dozens were injured seriously enough to be taken to the hospital. Fortunately Handel took his own advice, stayed calm, and waited until he could get safely off the train. Still, he did not feel he could justify going home. Instead he began the journey to work on foot. The three-and-a-half-mile walk through freezing rain and snow took him four hours, but he made it to his job.

E. E. Handel was not alone in his fear of losing his job. Mollie Katz, a single woman in her midthirties, braved the elements to take the elevated train from Manhattan to the office where she worked as a clerk. Mollie boarded the train at 7:30 A.M. to find it already crowded with workers frantically trying to reach their

Ice, snow, and low visibility caused train cars to become stranded along elevated sections of track like that shown here. In at least one instance, entrepreneurial types propped a ladder against a trestle and charged passengers 15¢ to descend from a stranded train.

jobs. She clung to an overhead strap and tried to maintain her balance as the train moved in fits and starts along the track. When it entered a long curve near Third Street, the train came to a dead stop. Minutes turned into an hour. Because most people in the 1880s not only didn't bathe every day but also wore their clothes several times between washes, it wasn't surprising that the air in the crowded train quickly became stale. Then, to add to the general discomfort, the engineer turned off the steam, cutting the only heat source. The passengers were torn between keeping windows shut for warmth and opening them for fresh air. Mollie later remembered men frantically pushing windows and roof trapdoors open, "looking for ladders or some other way out of their trap." Every time they opened a window, the storm rushed in, driving snow and freezing wind throughout the car.

With most passengers standing, the hours passed slowly. People with sack lunches began to nibble at sandwiches. Finally rumor of a rescue passed through the car. Some of the braver and stronger men in the train had earlier climbed out windows and crawled along the ice-covered elevated track to the station. Now the men had returned with a ladder. They propped it against the trestle and offered it as a means of escape to anyone willing to pay 15¢. Mollie Katz climbed out of the train onto the track and watched the first men maneuver onto the ladder. "With so much snow and ice," she said later, "it was some stunt to . . . balance oneself on a tie or rail, then reach for the ladder ends, swing around and descend."

Hampered by her long skirt, which caught the blowing wind like a sail, Mollie decided not to try descending the ladder until an enterprising man tied another ladder onto the first to extend its reach. With the top rung even with the train tracks, Mollie became more courageous and swung herself onto the ladder. She learned later that many of the men and most of the women had declined to risk the descent by ladder and had waited until night, when another locomotive arrived to pull the cars back to the station.

While Mollie's decision to attempt the ladder was certainly urged on by the rising winds and dropping temperatures—plus the fact that she hadn't eaten all day—she might also have heard a rumor that had spread throughout the train. Apparently a mathematically inclined passenger had estimated that on the downtown track there were at least 80 trains, consisting of five cars each, with an average of 100 passengers in each car. He calculated that the passengers, most of whom were men, weighed on average 150 pounds each. That added up to 3,000 tons of human beings—plus the weight of the cars, engines, and snow—all pressing on the outside rail of the curved section of track. The amateur mathematician thought it likely that the enormous weight would overwhelm the structure supporting the tracks, sending the trains toppling to the ground. Fear of being crushed in such an accident may have been the final nudge Mollie needed to try the ladder.

Stockbrokers such as Edward D. Jones (later of Dow-Jones fame) started the day similarly but ended on a much different note. Jones left his comfortable home in Harlem, a middle-class neighborhood in Manhattan, on the elevated train. Four hours later—and still very far from Wall Street—he and a group of fellow stockbrokers called it a day. They booked rooms in a fine hotel nearby and ordered a substantial lunch to take the edge off their strenuous morning. These men were fortunate that they didn't have to worry about losing their jobs. Other, perhaps less senior, members of Wall Street firms paid as much as $40 for a horse-drawn cab ride to work. On a normal day the fare would have been just $1.

This is not to say that all prosperous citizens stayed home or checked into a comfortable hotel. Theodore Roosevelt, the future U.S. president, walked three miles in the blowing storm to keep an appointment of no great importance. Of course, Roosevelt was probably wearing a fur coat and hat, lined gloves, and thick clothes underneath it all.

Few workingmen had such luxurious clothing. As the weather worsened, clothing assumed a new level of importance in every person's life. Women had the most difficult time, being forced to contend with long skirts, high heels, and hats with veils that quickly caked with ice. One enterprising young store clerk invented a new kind of wool pull-on cap by cutting bathing suit trunks through the center and tying each leg with a string. These quickly sold out, as did all of the winter's leftover earmuffs. Rubber thigh-boots meant for fishing also sold briskly. Those who could not afford, or find, extra winter clothing improvised by stuffing newspapers inside their shirts.

While the inhabitants of New York City faced the additional challenge of moving about a large area between home and work, the weather was actually worse elsewhere, something even Sergeant Long, a survivor of years trapped on the Arctic tundra, would have found hard to imagine. After the storm was over, he said that he had "never seen wind or cold like there was in New York that Monday."

"Cut Off"

The blizzard isolated towns and cities alike. To his chagrin, President Grover Cleveland discovered that even the nation's capital was completely cut off.

3

"Cut Off," read the headline of the *Boston Globe*. Most northeasterners understood the feeling Monday after the storm arrived. Journalists across the affected states would have heartily agreed with their colleagues at the *Globe* as well. As the storm raged, few reporters wanted to brave the ice and cold in search of stories. Because of this, most of the news was local: with telegraphs and telephones out of order, with trains and ferries at a standstill, no news traveled between towns.

Even the president of the United States, Grover Cleveland, found himself isolated. Cleveland and his wife were at their country house near Washington, D.C., and learned of the storm when a gigantic elm fell in the backyard, awakening them from their sleep. The president was upset to find that the nation's capital was cut off from the rest of the country. In fact,

High winds and heavy snows downed telegraph and telephone poles, silencing the high-speed communication that Americans during the so-called Age of Confidence had begun to take for granted.

Washington was so isolated by the storm that an invading army could have arrived from the south and no one would have been the wiser for days. For a short time news managed to reach the capital through a roundabout process that, ironically, relied upon the longest distance: the underwater cable connecting the United States with Europe. The only other cable that withstood the ice and high winds was the Washington-Chicago line. While this cable held, news could reach Boston newspapers from Washington, D.C., if sent first from Washington to Chicago, then from Chicago to London, England, then from London to Boston.

Communication between smaller towns was equally difficult. Telegraph operators had to work hard to find a connection between towns that would circumvent fallen lines. Operators rerouted messages over increasingly longer and more complicated routes until finally too many lines were down. Just as Washington, D.C., relied upon the transatlantic line for its information, other places had to send messages through Montreal, Canada, in order to reach neighboring towns. Finally Montreal was unable to cope with the volume of traffic, and no more messages were transmitted along that line, sending entire states into isolation.

Even sending messages within a town presented a problem. Western Union delivery boys strapped long wires around their waist, hoping that if they ended up stranded in a snowdrift, rescuers would have a way to pull them out.

Although the loss of telegraph service constituted a serious problem for those with businesses to run, most people didn't use cables every day. Mail service was more essential. But the mail wasn't getting through either. Even if local letter carriers could brave the wind, cold, and snow, the intercity trains that delivered mail were stuck in drifts, leaving few letters to deliver. Normally, mail service in the 1880s was quite dependable. Letters sent between cities in the northeastern states typically reached their destination within a day or two. The blizzard stretched delivery time to a week, striking a hard blow to postmen who prided themselves on completing their appointed rounds despite rain, sleet, or snow. Probably because of this pride in their work, postmen weren't willing to give up without trying. In Brooklyn, for example, the letter carriers slogged through the deep snow only to find businesses closed and unable to receive the mail. More than 20 postmen in Brooklyn alone had to be rescued from drifts. Finally it was clear that mail service had to be discontinued until the storm passed.

The telephone was another means of communication disrupted by the storm. Introduced only a decade before, telephones had caught on quickly, though they were still found mostly at businesses and in the homes of the wealthy. Nevertheless, numerous telephone lines added to the bundles of cable and electric wire crisscrossing the urban landscape.

During the storm, telephone operators—called

"In all my experience, I have never had so many calls to answer, nor so many cranks to deal with," a telephone operator in Worcester, Massachusetts, said of her shift during the blizzard. That phone customers may have been a little irritable is small wonder: many waited for hours before operators connected their calls.

operatives—had a particularly difficult time. In the 1880s, there was no direct dialing; all calls had to be connected by an operative. Fifteen operatives were on the job in Worcester, Massachusetts, when the storm hit. Over the next hours they received three times the normal volume of calls, mostly from people desperate to get word on stranded trains. As hard as they tried, the operatives couldn't answer all the calls quickly; some callers had to wait on the line for hours before finally getting through. The result was irate callers and frazzled operatives. After the storm, one operative was quoted in the *Worcester Daily Telegram*. "In all my experience," she said, "I have never had so many calls to answer, nor so many cranks to deal with. Your reporters have a good deal to say concerning sleepy operatives and operatives' neglect; but one hour in this exchange this afternoon would convince you that the operatives themselves are the real sufferers."

In Hartford, Connecticut, the city's telephone system remained relatively intact throughout the storm, allowing frantic callers to telephone grocers with demands for overdue deliveries. The same telephone line—the only link between Hartford and Boston—allowed the local paper to report on events outside the city.

Across the northeastern states people were unsure how far the storm damage stretched. Equally disturbing was that they didn't know how long the storm would last. And while some problems were shared by almost everyone—no electricity, no telephone, no cables, no mail, no trains or ferries—some people found themselves in unique predicaments.

In Liberty, New York, a young farmer struggled to his barn to find his cows still alive and standing, albeit buried up to their heads in snow. After digging all six of them out, the farmer traipsed across his fields in search of other strange snow scenes. Few people of the time had cameras, but this man did, and he recorded some of the spectacles he encountered. He may have considered the railway station a remarkable sight with its roof blown off, but the snowdrifts were the most amazing part of the winter landscape. One drift stood so high that the farmer was able to stand on top of it and be at eye level with the chimney of a two-and-a-half-story house. Three months later, on a hot day in the middle of June, he photographed the very last clump of snow marking the once enormous drift.

While the storm dumped large quantities of precipitation on some areas, in other places it created a lack of usable water. With little snowfall in Washington, the problem was record low temperatures and powerful winds. At low tide the high winds blew most of the water out of the Potomac River, and what little remained froze rapidly. In fact, conditions on the river changed so fast that commuter ferries between the riverbanks became stuck in the mud on the river bottom. This quick freeze allowed brave—or foolhardy—souls to walk across the frozen bottom to the opposite shore.

Camden, New Jersey, suffered a similar problem, but the effects were more widespread. As on the Potomac, high winds struck the Delaware River at low tide, blowing the water out of the riverbed and stopping all ferry traffic between Camden and Philadelphia. Ferries that were already on the river scraped bottom and got stuck. One ferry was grounded in the middle of the channel, stranding the passengers between the two ports for the duration of the storm. While this was a critical problem for those needing to travel to and from work, the city quickly realized that low water was going to be a hardship for all residents of Camden.

Most problematic was drinking water. All of Camden received its drinking water from a system of pumps along the Delaware River. The pumps pulled water from near the river bottom because that's where the current ran the strongest and, presumably, the water was the freshest. During the storm, the water level fell below the mouths of the pumps. Although city residents could obtain drinking water by melting snow—which was found in abundance—the failure of the pump system made them realize the frailty of the city's water system.

To make matters worse, the Pennsylvania Railroad and several other local industries used river water to run their steam plants. All across town plants faced the same problem: the river level was too low to draw water for their machinery. The Pennsylvania Railroad soon realized that it didn't need steam power, as snow and ice on

Pedestrians take refuge under the roof of a row of stores.

the tracks were blocking its engines. Other local industries, such as the local newspaper, were forced to suspend or cut back on work when they couldn't obtain the water necessary for their steam-powered equipment. In an era without work-related insurance, a closed factory wasn't a holiday for the worker and his or her family; it meant no pay for many who desperately needed every penny.

The situation was even worse at factories located in more remote areas. In Elizabeth, New Jersey, home to the Singer factory, workers arrived by a short train ride every day. On the Monday of the storm nearly two-thirds of the workforce—1,800 people—showed up to earn their pay.

Kenny Dilts was among them. After the reduced workforce started production, however, word spread that because the coal train couldn't get through, the plant would have to close. Like the factories in Camden, the Singer factory ran all its equipment on steam. Unlike the Camden factories, it had water, but no coal meant no way to transform the water into steam. Faced with idling machinery, the factory managers decided to send home the workers—who had barely had a chance to warm themselves after the hard trip in—to avoid paying for a day of unproductive labor. The prospect of another trip in the blizzard wearing long skirts and high-heeled boots convinced many of the female employees to refuse to leave the factory. But Kenny Dilts and most of the men walked the quarter mile to the railroad station, trusting that a passenger train would take them back to town.

They left the factory in groups of 20 or more, hoping to stay warmer and not get lost. Dilts found himself sep-

CIVIC DUTY VERSUS THE STORM

In New Hampshire the second Monday of March was the day set aside for annual town meetings. Established during colonial times in order to get all landowners involved in local government, the annual meetings had been fixed by state law. The meetings revolved around important local issues such as the town budget, tax rates, and candidates for town council. While the stated purpose of the meetings was clearly official, the yearly gatherings also afforded people the opportunity to exchange news and see old friends. Because the harsh winter months prevented traveling, by March people were generally anxious to go to town, and the weather usually cooperated. The annual meetings lasted well into the night, and the women of the town traditionally provided dinner.

As luck would have it, the storm arrived on the very day of the yearly Monday meetings. While many residents couldn't or didn't leave home to make the difficult trip, some did, braving snow higher than the backs of their horses. In Tilton, New Hampshire, a man named George H. Brown was cited by the town clerk as the bravest voter for his trek into town.

arated from the group and struggling to find his way only minutes after they had stepped into the blowing snow and ice. As he trudged through the snowdrifts, he met a man who had left before him. The man's face was covered with ice and his eyelids were frozen shut. Sightless, the man stumbled around, unable to find his way. Dilts caught up to the man as he fell into a drift. He broke the ice from the man's face, but because the man was confused, Dilts had to shake and hit him until the man was roused enough to continue the struggle to the station. After passing other men in the same condition, Dilts was not surprised to learn that several men never made it to the station. Later he commented, "I do not doubt that they are buried in the drifts."

All across the northeastern states the effects of the storm were striking. Trains were stranded across the countryside. Near the top of Manhattan was a particularly bad stretch of railroad known to railroaders as Spike. Spike was officially called the Spuyten Duyvil railroad cut, 150 feet deep, 500 feet long, and curved. The danger usually lay in the fact that it was such a long curve. If a train stopped in it for any reason, engineers on approaching trains couldn't see the stopped train until they were almost upon it, and a collision often resulted.

At 6:40 Monday morning the Croton local, one engine pulling seven commuter-filled coaches, hit a high snowdrift at the northern mouth of the cut and ground to a halt. Behind the Croton local was the eight-coach Peekskill local, which also hit a drift and stopped. Behind that were two sleeper trains from the West. Soon eight trains were stalled one behind the other, and there they remained for three days.

Samuel M. Davis, a telegraph operator who lived near the cut, left his job when he realized that the telegraph wire was down. Davis went home and told his wife

In one respect the people shown here are lucky: the horsecar in which they were traveling has become stranded in front of a hotel. During the blizzard stranded travelers packed hotels to overflowing, with some guests even sleeping in bathtubs.

and mother that sandwiches and coffee were needed to feed a lot of stranded passengers. While his wife and mother started baking bread, Davis went to the local grocery store and bought everything he could find that might go on a sandwich. Together Davis, his wife, and his mother assembled 300 sandwiches and brewed three iron kettles of coffee. They, along with other locals, fed the stranded passengers until the snow was plowed on Wednesday.

Boston received less snow than many cities, but the residents of Beantown saw a great deal of rain and sleet. In addition to the downed telegraph poles and stranded trains that other communities faced, Boston suffered a pounding by the Atlantic Ocean. But while Boston's papers were running ominous headlines like "Cut Off," it took more than a blizzard to disturb the editor of a small weekly newspaper published in southern Rhode Island. In the week after the storm the small weekly paper noted that there had been something of a snowstorm and "horrible traveling" all week. However, the editor saw a definite bright spot: the weather had driven the birds out of the woods, and rose-breasted grosbeaks had been spotted.

More rural than urban, small towns didn't face the problems large cities did. The people in small towns were closer to the food supply than were city dwellers. They were also less likely to have, and therefore be dependent on, city water, electricity, or heat. While many residents of small towns found it just as important to reach work, they had shorter distances to travel, making them less likely to take trains or ferries every day. Instead they walked; dressed warmly and sure of the terrain, they had a chance.

In the small town of Bellows Falls, Vermont, houses were nearly buried by the snowdrifts. The drifts were so high, in fact, that they covered the windows, leaving only the chimneys to mark where the houses stood. Even the town's two-story hotel was buried in a high drift. Hotel employees worked hard to dig a tunnel to the front door, allowing stranded travelers to find a place to wait out the storm.

Philadelphia was harder hit by the storm than Boston. High winds pushed a brand-new smokestack, 140 feet tall, to the ground. Flagpoles flew through the sky, as did plate-glass windows and roofs. Reports of people being picked up and tossed through the air were not uncommon. A druggist walking past a police station was picked up and blown inside, where he landed at the sergeant's desk. At a railroad station a boy who sold papers and candy was blown off the platform in front of an oncoming train. The alert engineer stopped the train in the nick of time. The boy was returned to the station platform, unhurt but unhappy because he had lost his hat and a basket of candies.

Despite the severe weather, the *Philadelphia Bulletin*, unlike other newspapers, refused to sensationalize. Desperate for news, some papers, particularly those in isolated towns, printed frightening rumors—for example, that a big fire at Stamford, Connecticut, had left the railroad in ashes and most of the town ablaze, or that the Brighton Hotel at Coney Island had blown into the ocean, taking the guests with it. Refusing to print rumors, however, the Tuesday edition of the *Bulletin* spoke of "the most disagreeable snow storm of the season." Most of the news stories revolved around stranded travelers. Hotels were filled to overflowing with strangers sharing every nook and cranny of available space. Beds were hastily made out of spare linens in halls and bathtubs. Most of the stranded travelers were so happy to be inside away from the cold that they didn't complain. And entertainment wasn't necessarily too far away. Traveling theatrical groups, circus performers, and musicians were usually more than willing to share their talents.

While the *Philadelphia Bulletin* held to its standards of accurate reporting, real damage was done by the more dramatic stories reported by papers like the *Albany Journal*. A reporter trying to follow up on the Brighton Hotel story hired a horse and carriage to visit the site. The report of the hotel blowing into the sea turned out to be false, but the reporter did meet with disaster. He was found the next day, frozen in place on the carriage seat—still holding the reins.

While desperate factory workers braved miles of cold roads on foot, and stranded travelers made the best of the situation and encouraged their companions in impromptu performances, the members of the state senate in Albany, New York, fared less well. Only 7 of 50 legislators reported for work on the Monday of the storm. Although the snow reached record depths in Albany—up to 50 inches in places—many citizens of New York City were later ill pleased by the senators' performance. After all, these were the same senators who had refused money to New York City for improvements like underground subways and buried electrical wires. When the official record of the senators' remarks on the storm became public, opinion fell even lower. Apparently even the senators who made the trip to the capitol building still did not understand how severe the effects of the storm had been up and down the coast. If they had known that babies in New York City had died because the milk trains couldn't reach the city, or that scores of people had frozen while walking to work after the commuter trains and ferries failed, or that even more had frozen in their apartments when the coal trains didn't deliver fuel, would they have been so unconcerned? Cold, failed transportation, loss of communication, starvation caused by interrupted food delivery, and flooding caused by melting snow—these were the problems that the legislators would eventually have to deal with once the storm had cleared and the snow had melted.

Blizzard at
Sea

Up and down the east coast, harrowing conditions confronted sailors during the blizzard.

4

A young *New York World* reporter named William O. Inglis, eager to prove his worth, had jumped at the chance to write a feature story on the life of harbor pilots. These sailors made their living guiding large ships into the harbor. Because the first pilot boat to reach an incoming ship gained the right to escort it—and collect the fee—pilot-boat captains raced one another with reckless abandon. Over the years, these races had resulted in enough collisions to make harbor pilots famous for their daring. In the view of the young reporter, tagging along on a pilot boat was bound to yield a fascinating newspaper story.

So on Saturday, March 10, Inglis made arrangements to sail out of New York harbor aboard the pilot boat *Caldwell F. Colt*. Although the weather was fair, Inglis was a bit anxious. In his zeal to make a good impression on his new editor, he had neglected to mention the fact that he was prone to seasickness. He even got queasy on a short ferry ride. Nonetheless, Inglis believed he might be spared that fate on this journey, for the sea air was refreshing, the skies clear, and the prospect of making a dash out of the harbor exciting. To keep his mind off his stomach, the reporter paid close attention to the pilots and asked numerous questions about their job.

Saturday was traditionally the busiest day for ocean-going vessels in and out of New York harbor. On that particular Saturday eight transatlantic vessels set sail, and nine pilot schooners left to escort the 19 ships that were due in over the weekend. The *Colt,* the pilot schooner on which Inglis had chosen to sail, was an 85-foot, two-masted vessel that carried five pilots, a boat keeper, a steward, and four men before the mast. Inglis quickly understood how fierce the competition was among the pilot boats as they made their way out of the harbor and into open water. He watched as the eight other pilot boats maneuvered into position, each trying to spot the arriving big ships first. The pilot in command of the *Colt,* James Fairgreaves, explained to Inglis that whenever large ships were expected, the pilot boats made their way downriver and out to Sandy Hook, where they waited. When they sighted an arriving ship, they hoisted sail and made a dash toward her, hoping to win the race and claim the escort fee. It was the race for the ships that made the job dangerous and a worthwhile news story in the eyes of the *New York World.*

As they sailed out to sea, Fairgreaves pointed out other vessels to Inglis, including the fellow pilot boat *Enchantress.* The oldest pilot boat in service, *Enchantress* wasn't the fastest, but she was reliable. However, Inglis's eye was caught by another, sleeker vessel. Fairgreaves identified her as *Cythera,* a handsome new yacht bound

for the Caribbean on her maiden voyage. While some of the seamen around Inglis muttered about the danger of "landlubbers" in their fancy yachts, the reporter couldn't help but admire *Cythera*'s sleek lines, and he was glad to hear the grudging admission that she was being handled well as she sailed past the *Colt*.

Once on the Atlantic, the *Colt* turned southward, hoping to catch New York–bound vessels along the New Jersey coast between the towns of Atlantic Highlands and Cape May. They passed several ships that declined pilots, including the *Iroquois* and *Sunlight,* before Inglis decided to call it a night. Although he was not as seasick as he had feared, Inglis's stomach had begun to play tricks on him. Just before turning in on Saturday night, he wrote: "The evening was clear and had every promise of fair weather.

A section of New York's busy harbor, late 1800s. On the weekend the blizzard began, 19 trans-atlantic ships were due to arrive at the harbor.

Yachts in Marblehead Harbor, Massachusetts, 1888. The unexpected storm took amateur and professional sailors alike by surprise, and in an era in which many vessels were powered by sail alone, the danger was greatly magnified.

The sea kept taking liberties with our boat, though, and I lost interest in the marine landscape."

The same day that Inglis had joined the pilot boats in New York, other landlubbers in the small town of Lewes, Delaware, were enjoying the sea on a fine spring day. Situated at the mouth of the Delaware Bay, Lewes was a favorite summer spot among vacationers because of its beaches and pretty town. During the winter months, however, it drew mostly seamen. On Saturday, March 10, a young divinity student from Princeton University, John H. Marshall, was visiting to preach in the local Presbyterian church. When Marshall joined his host, the local minister, for dinner, a light rain was falling and the sea was gray and choppy. The day was still nice enough for a walk, however, and the two men took a turn through town. After the evening service, the walk to the minister's house was not as pleasant, for it was raining harder and the wind was blowing from the southeast in gusts. To Marshall, content after a productive day and a fine meal, the wind and rain only made his host's house feel cozier as they went to bed.

Around midnight the divinity student was startled from his sleep by a commotion outside his window. "To the pier! Hurry! To the pier!" voices shouted.

Marshall dressed quickly and met his host downstairs. Both men then joined other townspeople on the beach road that led to the long wooden pier inside the breakwater (an offshore wall constructed parallel to the beach to protect it from waves).

The scene had changed completely since Marshall's afternoon walk. Whereas the gray sea had been serene, if ominous, in the afternoon, even a landsman could now tell that disaster was near. The wind was blowing so hard that Marshall had to struggle to remain standing, and the heavy, driving snow made it difficult to see by the flickering lantern light. Nevertheless, what Marshall could make out horrified him: the ships that had been lying peacefully at anchor in the harbor had been caught unprepared by the storm. Some of the ships were beached, while others were sinking; men screamed to be saved. Some sailors had already fallen into the icy water; others clung to masts and rigging, pitching back and forth as the ships rolled with the high wind and waves.

With little time for idle talk, a local man explained to Marshall and the minister what had happened. Apparently just before midnight the wind had swung around unexpectedly from the southeast to the north and then changed again to the northwest. The shift was so sudden and strong that anchor chains broke under the pressure. Even before the seamen could respond to the warning "All hands on deck," the damage was irreparable. With anchor chains broken and masts snapped like twigs in the wind, steamers, schooners, and tugs were driven into one another. Several crashed into the wooden pier, and the tug *Lizzie V. Crawford* rammed straight through it, snapping the heavy timbers before being driven up onto the beach.

Rescue operations continued throughout the night despite dark, cold, and snow. The moaning of the wooden ships was occasionally punctuated by a crack as beams broke. Men—and at least one woman, for the captain of the *George Simpson* had his wife aboard—called out for help as their ships sank. The captain's wife was both brave and lucky. She waited for the exact moment when the crashing waves brought the deck of her husband's sinking ship even with the deck of the tug *Protector,* then jumped to safety. Many were not so fortunate. The *George Simpson*'s mate and one crewman were thrown into the frigid sea. They were pulled to seeming safety by some of the *Tamesei*'s crew. Unfortunately, what they thought was safety was only a part of the broken pier. Over the next five or six hours they and nine other men were stranded in the dark, with waves crashing over them and temperatures dropping.

When daylight broke, Marshall found the "wild sight" even more frightening. The pier was severed in three places, and the 11 men on the broken end were stranded 500 yards from shore. The waves were so violent that a rescue attempt by boat was ruled out. Marshall and the others watched helplessly as the stranded men stood still to prevent their delicate perch from collapsing—despite the fact that their clothing was frozen solid and the cold was only getting worse. Even more discouraging, word was passed that the crews of both local lifesaving stations, Lewes and Cape Henlopen, were already busy several miles down shore, where 14 schooners and several steam freighters had run aground. This meant no help

was coming for hours. Upon hearing this, a cold and tired John Marshall realized that he was ill equipped to give any real assistance. In fact, he was in the way. So on Sunday afternoon he trudged to the railway station and boarded a two-car train to return to Princeton.

As John Marshall boarded the train, William Inglis was in his bunk on the pilot boat *Colt*. His stomach had finally gotten the best of him. The chief pilot, James Fairgreaves, had assured the reporter that what seemed like rough weather was really only a wave or two whipped up by a brisk southeast breeze. But neither this assurance nor the prospect of seeing the *Enchantress* again could get Inglis out of his bunk on Sunday.

John Marshall was having a difficult time on Sunday as well. In blinding snow and swirling wind, his train

On the deck of a harbor pilot ship, which guided large oceangoing vessels in and out of America's harbors.

had left Lewes carrying only five passengers along with the crew. Only a few miles out of the station the locomotive plowed into a snowdrift as high as the train cars, coming to a screeching stop. The prospect of being stuck in the train for a prolonged period was decidedly unappealing, but Marshall, his four fellow passengers, and the crew had already experienced enough of the storm to realize that attempting to walk back to the station would be foolhardy.

Although Marshall may have wished himself anywhere but trapped in a train car, he probably would not have traded places with William Inglis. The train car was cold and drafty and they didn't have much food to share, but those difficulties paled beside the problems aboard the pilot boat *Colt*.

Inglis was asleep in his bunk at 11:30 A.M. on Monday when a big swell hit the schooner solidly under the bow, or front end, and lifted her upward. The reporter wakened as the boat reeled backward like a fighter who has absorbed a heavy punch to the jaw. While she was hanging in the air, a second wave caught the *Colt* on the side, capsizing her. Inside the cabin everything was thrown to the floor. Inglis held fast to his bunk as the boat shuddered from the pressure of the waves. On deck the scene was chaos: despite being near noon, it was as dark as midnight. The topmasts were under water, the lifeboats inaccessible. Suddenly the bow of the ship shifted up into the air, leaving the *Colt* standing on her stern, or back end. Seawater poured into the main hatch, rushing through the boat. Crew members fought their way through the freezing, swirling water to the deck, which was pointing straight up to the sky. Too scared to be sick, Inglis clung to the post of his bunk, his legs dangling helplessly. He was astounded when the boat suddenly heaved forward and righted herself against the waves.

On deck the crew assembled, working the pumps and trying to save the ship. Below deck Inglis was only slightly heartened by the cook, who seemed as concerned about losing a good soup as he was about the ship's sinking. Inglis realized that the cook was trying to cheer him up, and it would take a miracle to see them safely to shore. The entire cabin was awash with cold seawater, the sails were ripped, and the men quickly grew exhausted in the wind and cold. What had started out as a story about the dangerous daily life of the pilot boat had taken a far darker turn.

Up and down the shore, lifesaving crews and ships' crews were hard at work. Official lifesaving stations had been in existence on the dangerous coast since 1871, and they were getting a full workout. As soon as they were able, the crews near Lewes moved into town and the wrecked harbor. Although they worked as fast as possible, it was nearly night when they turned their attention to the men on the broken pier. Trained for such disasters, the lifesaving crews fired line out to the castaways, then started the dangerous mission of sending a boat out along the line to bring the men ashore. Altogether 40 men were rescued by the Lewes and Cape Henlopen lifesaving stations that day. At the Lewes hospital 17 seamen were treated. One lost his mind; others were maimed for life as a result of the cold. But none would have survived had it not been for the bravery of the lifesaving crews.

All along the eastern seashore the storm brought danger. At Newport, Rhode Island, the chief of the lifesaving station reported that the sea was the worst he had ever experienced. Huge waves crashed across the breakwaters, and visibility was restricted. But danger and hardship at sea were not limited to the Atlantic coastal waters. The rivers feeding the coast turned treacherous as well.

Manhattan, New York City's most famous borough,

is surrounded by the East River and the Hudson River. The East River, really more of a tidal inlet than a river, and the Hudson, really a fjord, were both busy as usual on the weekend the storm arrived. Square-rigged sailing ships, fishing schooners, yachts, oyster sloops, and, of course, pilot boats like the *Colt* were sailing up and down the rivers or were tied alongside the wharves.

Adding to the activity were the ferries operating 35 lines, 18 of them between Manhattan and outlying areas. These ferries were the lifelines of the workforce that flowed between Manhattan and Brooklyn, Coney Island, and Staten Island. Since the rivers were saltwater inlets, they did not freeze as the temperatures dropped. However, as the storm raged on Monday, disaster struck the ferries caught unexpectedly in midstream. The mid-morning ferry from Staten Island, filled with passengers, nearly collided with the schooner *Mary Heitman,* which was blowing downriver, dragging both of her anchors. Aboard the schooner were five crewmen but no captain. With its rigging and sails covered in ice, the *Mary Heitman* was completely out of control. After the near miss with the ferry, she was swept out into the Lower Bay, where she collided with a three-masted schooner. As the two ships locked, one of the crewmen from the *Mary Heitman* jumped to the other ship. He was lucky: before the others could follow, the ships parted and the *Mary Heitman* blew farther out to sea. Neither the ship nor the remaining four crewmen were ever seen again.

Alfred E. Smith, age 14 the year of the blizzard, lived with his mother near the Manhattan entrance to the Brooklyn Bridge, within sight of the East River. When he looked out the window on Tuesday morning, the river appeared frozen. In fact, it was clogged with a patchwork of ice floes that had floated in from the Upper New York Bay with the night tide. One enormous chunk stretched unbroken from Brooklyn to Manhattan. Wider than the river, it jammed against piers and marooned ferries in their slips as it moved. Smith knew what the watermen called such an ice floe: a harbormaster. Clearly this harbormaster wasn't going to permit ferryboat commuters to cross the river.

To his amazement, however, young Al Smith watched a steady stream of pedestrians, dogs—even a man on horseback—cross the river on the ice. Icebound fishermen brought their ladders out and made money charging people for assistance climbing up and down the icy banks.

To people who needed to get to and from work, it may have seemed that crossing the river in this manner was a good idea. In reality, though, this crossing was much more treacherous than it looked. The river wasn't really frozen—it was a patchwork of ice floes jammed together by the tide. When the tide turned, the ice floes would shift, break apart, and float out to sea, from where they had come.

Years after the great snowstorm, Alfred E. Smith, governor of New York and the 1928 Democratic nominee for president, cofounded the Society of Blizzard Men.

Experienced seamen understood the dangers more than most. Always alert to the shifting waters, they tried to warn people. But when the tide began to turn around 9:45 A.M., many were too excited about the prospect of crossing the river to listen to the warning. By 10:00 the tide had shifted the ice noticeably. More than 100 people were still crossing when the edges of the ice floe scraped against shore, signaling a massive movement. The sound of ice scraping metal and wood caused a panic, and most of the people began to run for shore. But more than 40 were still on the ice when it began floating away. It drifted slowly seaward, and as it moved, the edges softened, making them impossible to stand on. Suddenly those still on the floe could not walk to the edges and jump to shore. Hoping for a miracle, the remaining 40 crowded on the edge nearest land, some joking, a few praying. One man shouted that he would cable from Europe. Just as tugs were maneuvering near to attempt a rescue, the floe grated to a stop along the Mallory Pier. Though it remained in place for only five minutes, that was enough time for 40 frightened pedestrians to scramble ashore to safety.

On the other side of Manhattan the story almost took a grimmer turn. Several people trapped on ice floes were moving steadily away from shore. Two men were each trapped on ice patches only as big as doormats. A tug spotted them, came alongside, and plucked the men off with ropes before they capsized. Thousands of people on the riverside screamed their approval at the daring rescue.

On Tuesday, with the worst of the storm over, more and more people ventured outside, trying to dig their way out, find their way to work, or simply enjoy the sights of a world covered in white. Young Al Smith was one such person. Buried by snow inside his mother's house from Sunday until Tuesday morning, he was happy to make his way outside again. Years later, as a Democratic presidential candidate, he would tell and retell the story of those blustery winter days and the people walking across the East River.

William Inglis and John Marshall would also get the opportunity to tell and retell their stories. But as Al Smith shoveled his way clear of his mother's house on Tuesday morning, Inglis still harbored doubts that he would live to touch dry land again. On Tuesday night the winds had died down, but the *Colt* remained far out to sea and would have to pass through ice floes before reaching shore. Fairgreaves, the chief pilot, remarked that in 34 years of sailing all over the world he had never seen such a storm.

As they neared the bay Wednesday morning, they saw graphic evidence of the storm's power. Half-sunk schooners dotted the water. Other, luckier vessels were being towed in by tugs. Still other ships were caught in the ice, their crews as yet unsure of the full extent of the damage. Nearing shore, the crew of the *Colt* sat down for their first hot meal since Sunday night. While they were seated, the captain of a passing tug called news down to them. Nine pilot boats had been wrecked, he said. Among them were boats Inglis knew. Both *Enchantress* and *William H. Starbuck* had vanished at sea. Also lost with all hands was the beautiful yacht *Cythera*.

Inland, the train carrying John Marshall was shoveled free on Wednesday. It had been sitting on the tracks since leaving Lewes on Sunday afternoon. Marshall's attitude about the storm he had just experienced was probably much different from the opinion of the captain who stepped ashore from the ship *Slavonia*. The captain and his ship were from the Baltic port of Stettin, located in the icy north seas of Europe. When asked to remark about the weather, the captain shrugged and said, "Only the usual winter weather."

Perhaps for him, but for the majority of sea captains that week the winter weather was far from usual.

Getting
There

A lone horse-drawn carriage in the distance is all the traffic on this thoroughfare. By the end of the blizzard even horses couldn't get through many city streets.

5

Most people living in America in 1888 had a clear idea of what life on the farm entailed. Cities had grown so rapidly in the previous decade that many city residents had at one time lived in the country. Other city dwellers still had relatives on farms or in small towns. The rise in the number of factory jobs brought about by the industrial revolution meant that there was a large group of first-generation city dwellers in America. This was also true of immigrants from Europe. While some of the immigrants came from the industrial towns of England and Germany, many had fled a difficult and uncertain life on the farm.

Farming, always an important part of American life, was difficult in the 19th century. Without heavy machinery to assist in the plowing of fields or maintenance of livestock, most farms were small operations, family run with a few hired hands. Even vegetable farmers usually had some livestock—a cow for the family's milk, chicken or pigs for Sunday dinner—and those animals, no matter how few, required year-round care. When the Blizzard of '88 hit, people in small towns and on farms had different problems from those of people living in the cities.

People living outside big cities were closer to food production, which meant they didn't go hungry when trains stopped delivering meat, milk, and vegetables to the frozen cities. They were also not dependent on electric lighting or coal-fired steam heating, as were occupants of the newer buildings in cities. Small-town and farm folk still relied almost exclusively on stoves for heating, and most families kept their winter supply of coal or wood stacked behind the house: a few days without delivery service wouldn't matter. With their oil lamps, woodstoves, and cellars full of potatoes and salted pork, three days of ice and snow were manageable. Of course, that didn't mean life in a storm was easy.

The young farmer in Liberty, New York, was lucky when he found his six cows buried but alive. He shoveled them out, gave them some extra hay, boarded up the hole in his barn so more snow wouldn't blow in, then took off to photograph interesting sights. Others were not so fortunate. The mild spring weather had caused some farmers to turn their livestock out into the fields. The suddenness of the storm, with its blowing snow and freezing temperatures, made it impossible to find all of the animals and bring them into barns. Many froze. Even more died because farmers couldn't reach their barns to feed and water them.

Of course, farmers had lived through winter storms before, and if this one came suddenly and on the eve of spring, that didn't change what had to be done. When Mrs. Chappelle woke to the sounds of a blizzard howling

outside her farmhouse near the village of Montville, Connecticut, in the Thames River valley, she certainly wasn't pleased. But she knew what to do. Her husband had spent the night a half mile away, across the field visiting his sick mother, so Mrs. Chappelle sent her two oldest sons, George and Alfred, to dig a path to the barn through the drifting snow. After this essential task was completed and the farm animals fed and watered, Mrs. Chappelle sent 16-year-old George across the snowy field with calf's-foot tea for his sick grandmother. Then she threw more wood on the fire and started the family's meal.

When George returned with word that his father now had a fever, Mrs. Chappelle's careful plans were overturned. She saw no alternative but to go nurse her husband and mother-in-law and leave her four sons alone to take care of the farm.

Although they generally didn't have to worry about obtaining food and fuel during the blizzard, as city dwellers did, farm families' relative isolation meant that they could be in serious trouble and neighbors would have no idea.

An engraving depicting the difficulties of getting around during the blizzard. With wind gusts topping 80 mph, the storm picked many people off the ground.

This in itself was not unusual. In the 19th century, even small children were routinely involved in day-to-day household chores. Children living in towns or cities delivered messages for their parents, fetched packages and groceries, and often held jobs after school. Boys growing up on a farm were also used as messengers when the distance wasn't too great, but more routinely they cared for livestock and worked in the fields alongside their father. Girls might be involved in these activities also, but they usually worked alongside their mother, learning to cook, clean, sew, and manage a household—the tasks they would be responsible for as adults. Because they had been helping out since a young age, Mrs. Chappelle felt confident that her oldest sons could manage the livestock without her.

As it turned out, it wasn't her oldest sons or the livestock that Mrs. Chappelle needed to worry about. With their mother absent and their older brothers less interested in entertaining them, the two younger boys— Gurton, age nine, and Legrand, age four—were bored. Because of the intense cold and blowing wind outside, they had been banned from helping with chores in the barn. Instead they were left to their own devices. They had popped the corn and eaten it all, then fought over the toys. Finally Gurton and Legrand amused themselves with the cat, which was also not happy about being inside all day. When that no longer amused the boys, they began whining, demanding that George play with them. Even though George had been across to his grandmother's and back, and had ventured out to feed the animals, he was as bored and irritable as his younger brothers. The younger boys' whining reached its peak while Alfred was in the barn tending the animals. Alone with his younger brothers, George reached his breaking point. He decided to go across the snowy field to his grandmother's and check on his parents. When the younger boys begged to come along, George was stern. "You stay right here and behave yourselves!" he admonished.

After he left, the house was just too quiet for young Legrand and Gurton, who were desperate for a little excitement. Only a few minutes passed before Gurton had an idea: he and Legrand would go across the field and surprise their parents. Legrand didn't hesitate, and both boys dressed warmly, as they had seen George do. Then they stepped out into the swirling snow. In their excitement they ran the first steps, then stopped and clung to each other. Usually they could see their grandmother's house across the field, but on this day the snow blotted out all the familiar landmarks. Even the gateposts of their yard had disappeared. Finally Gurton recognized a nearby elm tree and pulled his brother forward. Into the swirling snow they stumbled, aware now of how cold it was and how difficult it was to see even a few feet in front of their face, but no more able to see their own house than their grandmother's. On they trudged.

When Alfred finished caring for the animals and returned to the house, he was surprised to find all three of his brothers gone, but he assumed they had walked together to his grandmother's. Knowing that he was responsible for the animals in the barn, he stayed home. At the other end George had concluded that with Alfred in charge he didn't need to make the dangerous journey a third time in one day, so he decided to stay the night at his grandmother's. It wasn't until the next morning, when the storm let up a little and George returned on a sleigh, that anyone realized Gurton and Legrand were missing. Within an hour the alarm was up throughout the farming community, and a search party was organized.

So much snow had fallen since the previous afternoon, however, that there was no hope of finding the boys' tracks. Suspecting that the boys had become confused in the blinding storm, the search party fanned out across a large area between the two houses. When a neighbor discovered Legrand's cap and mittens near a huge snowdrift, the search party reassembled there. One neighbor believed they were near a stone wall, but with everything except the tallest landmarks buried beneath the snow, it was impossible to say for sure. To gauge the depth of the drift, he stuck a beanpole in the snow. "Ouch!" came a faint cry.

Frantically everyone began burrowing into the drift. In only a few minutes they uncovered Gurton, with his little brother leaning against him unconscious. The two boys had spent the afternoon, night, and most of the following morning—22 hours in all—in a little cave of snow against the stone wall 200 feet from their grand-mother's doorstep.

The boys were rushed back to their house, where their frozen clothes had to be cut off them. A neighbor who had spent his early years at sea in the north told the worried parents to immerse the boys in warm water to counteract hypothermia and frostbite. The boys didn't know it, but this bit of neighborly advice probably saved them. Many people who suffered from the cold during that blizzard were given a more common treatment: they were rubbed with snow. Along with the warm baths, the boys' mouths were pried open so whiskey could be administered. After the baths, at the suggestion of another neighbor, the boys were smeared with molasses and wrapped in sheets—an ineffective if harm-less treatment. Gurton and Legrand recovered and lived to old age, every winter telling the story of their night out in the great blizzard.

Not all stories ended as happily as Gurton and Legrand Chappelle's. In the countryside the relative iso-lation meant that people could be in trouble without any-one else even knowing about it. During the storm, children and adults alike became disoriented and froze to death while walking on normally familiar terrain. Ill-prepared families ran out of firewood and had no way of getting more.

People living in the city didn't have animals to feed and water, but they were just as dedicated when it came to going to work or school on the cold morning of Mon-day, March 12. Ten-year-old Rufus Billings, who lived on Nostrand Avenue in Brooklyn, insisted on going to school the morning of the storm. When his parents hid his boots to prevent him, he hunted until he found them, then rushed out the door. At school he found almost a dozen other eager children—but no teachers or janitor.

(continued on p. 74)

THE FINAL CASUALTY

Roscoe Conkling.

Roscoe Conkling decided to brave the blizzard on Monday, March 12, because he considered the trial that was scheduled to begin that day the most important civil case of the decade. The 58-year-old defense lawyer had already had an illustrious career. A three-term member of the U.S. House of Representatives who had gone on to serve two full terms in the Senate, Conkling had been mentioned as a potential presidential candidate in 1876 and 1880. His entire life had been a story of power and success, perhaps marred only by his temper and his inability to forget a grievance. After resigning from the Senate in protest of what he viewed as President Garfield's interference in New York politics, and after declining an appointment to the Supreme Court, Conkling returned to private law practice in New York City.

No one remembers how Conkling arrived at superior court in the midst of the city's worst blizzard, but arrive he did, bright and early Monday morning, ready for the trial. Conkling was disgusted when, after several hours' wait, he realized that no other attorneys were going to show up. Even worse, there was no judge. Angry, Conkling walked the short distance to his office, where he worked the rest of the day.

He was so busy that he didn't notice that the weather had gotten a lot worse. When he finally left after putting in a full day, a young attorney offered to find him a cab. But Conkling wouldn't pay the prices the weather-weary cabbies were charging, so he set off on foot. The young attorney joined Conkling for the first leg of his journey, then decided to stay the night at a hotel.

Conkling continued walking despite the darkness, driving snow, and falling temperatures. "I went magnificently along, shouldering through drifts and headed for the north," he told reporters the next day. Fortunately, Conkling was in excellent health, for he ate moderately, drank little, and worked out daily with barbells and punching bags. Still, he told reporters: "I was pretty well exhausted when I got to Union Square, and wiping the snow from my eyes, tried to make out the triangles there. But it was impossible. There was no light, and I plunged right on in as straight a line as I could. Sometimes I have run across passages in novels of great adventures in snow storms; for example, in stories of Russian life where there would be a vivid description of a man's struggle on a snow-swept and windy plain; I have always considered them exaggerations, but I shall never say so again. As a matter of fact, the strongest description would fail to approximate the truth."

The two-mile walk from his office to Union Square had taken Conkling two hours. Another hour later he was six blocks farther north at Madison Square. There he was forced to stop and melt the ice caked over his eyebrows and lashes with his hands so he could see to continue. Even so, he blundered into a high snowdrift. After a 20-minute struggle to free himself, Conkling continued to the New York Club at 25th Street. He collapsed on the doorstep of the club and had to be carried the short way to the hotel where he resided. The next day Conkling took a cab to his office and gave an account of his trip to reporters.

Unfortunately, Conkling had met his match in the storm. He left his office on Tuesday with a splitting earache and took to his bed. By the weekend he was extremely ill with pneumonia. During the first two weeks of April, some time after the storm, newspapers were filled with reports of Senator Conkling's illness. Bedridden since the week of the storm, he had been unable to shake off the pneumonia. On April 18 he died, the final casualty of the blizzard.

A cul-de-sac containing stores. People who fought their way through the snow in an attempt to buy supplies, like young Sam Strong, often found the stores closed.

(continued from p. 71)

The students stood outside the closed schoolhouse for nearly an hour before the principal arrived and formally dismissed them.

Just as dutiful was 10-year-old Sam Strong. An orphan, he lived with his aunt and uncle in Harlem. Sam's aunt, Mrs. Green, was expecting her dressmaker on Monday morning, which would mark the beginning of an annual ritual: a week spent inside the house making Mrs. Green's spring wardrobe. Readying the house for the dressmaker, Mrs. Green made a list of last-minute items they needed. Then, without looking outside, she told Sam to go to the store and buy them. When Sam mentioned that it was snowing, his aunt told him to wear his high rubber boots (a new invention) with his overcoat, wool cap, gloves, and muffler. She told him to hurry so he could finish the shopping before going to school. Accustomed—like many children in the 19th century—to running errands for the household, Sam knew that argument would only delay getting the job done. So he bundled up and headed out into the cold.

When Sam opened the front door, the storm nearly knocked him over. Sliding more than walking down the front steps, which were covered with a high drift of snow, he lowered his head and started for the store. Despite the difficulty of walking through waist-deep snowdrifts, Sam viewed the errand as an adventure—until he turned onto Lenox Avenue and came full face with the wind. The first gust carried him into the air and deposited him on a drift much higher than his head. After struggling to free himself, Sam received a warning from a passing policeman. Shouting through his ice-caked mustache to be heard over the wind, the policeman warned Sam that it was dangerous to be out walking in such bad weather. The policeman moved on, quickly vanishing from view in the windswept snow.

Despite the warning to return home, Sam continued. By this time he was determined to see his job through and buy thread and needles for his aunt. It wasn't until Sam reached the store and found it buried in snow up to the second-floor windows that he finally gave up.

The trip home was harder. Not only was Sam getting tired, but the snow was piling up faster and faster. He might have died if strangers hadn't pulled him out of snowdrifts a half dozen times. Even with this help, Sam arrived on the steps of his aunt and uncle's house a full four hours after setting out. Frantic with worry, his aunt and uncle were at the door to greet him. They pulled him up the steps and hurried to dry and warm him.

Years later Sam would remember always feeling that he had failed in his mission on the day of the blizzard. It was perhaps these strong memories that inspired him to later spend seven years researching a book to commemorate the 50th anniversary of the storm. By that time he was Dr. Sam Strong, and his book, *The Great Blizzard of 1888,* was the legacy of those who experienced, and remembered, the great storm.

Food and Fuel 6

The Blizzard of '88 struck people from all socioeconomic classes, but the poor—who often lacked such basic amenities as a warm house with hot water and adequate food—were particularly hard hit. Many immigrants in large cities like New York were likely to find themselves living in crowded apartment buildings called tenements. The New York Health Department had chosen a dumbbell-shaped floor plan for the majority of the buildings it operated. There were four apartments on each floor, two in each end of the dumbbell, with the connecting bar containing a hallway and toilet room with sink. None of the apartments built for poor families had running water in them; these families shared the common facilities in the hallway. Since many families were large, up to 40 people often shared one toilet and sink.

Just as there was no private running water in the apartments of the poor, those buildings also had only rudimentary heating and cooking facilities. Coal stoves and fireplaces served most buildings, and families bought their own coal and hauled it up the stairs to their apartment every day. During the blizzard the absence of a store of coal made the difference between life and death for many families. When the trains stopped delivering coal to the cities, only those with the money and space to have extra stored at home could continue to heat their homes and feed their stoves. People can go hungry for weeks without dying, but cold is much more dangerous. In many respects the coal shortage caused by the stalled trains was the most serious problem in the cities.

Fortunately, many people were kindhearted throughout the storm. A few coal dealers who were well supplied continued to sell at the normal rates. Some even gave coal to those who couldn't afford to buy any. On the Lower East Side of Manhattan the owner of a Russian-Turkish bath decided to close his business and give his coal to anyone who needed it.

However, not all were as public spirited. One West Eighth Street grocer charged a dollar for a pail of coal that normally cost 10¢, prompting someone to steal the wheels off the grocer's wagon and replace them with old ones. "Fair Exchange Is No Robbery," the thief chalked on the wagon—a clear message to the greedy grocer.

While freezing to death presented the greatest danger, hunger also worried many people. Their country cousins had stocked cellars to tide them over, but city living left little room for storage and even less money for such a luxury among the working class. Louis Fleischmann's Vienna Model Bakery, located on the corner of 10th Street and Broadway in New York, usually gave away leftover bread and rolls every evening. During the

blizzard the bakery stayed open all night, giving away baked goods to anyone who came by. Throughout Tuesday night long lines of men, women, and children wound around the block and back again waiting for their bread.

Meat was also hard to come by. Some butchers made their way to the market where the animals that had arrived by train before the storm were being held. If they could transport the beef to their store, the customers could be fed. Understandably, in a raging storm transportation was the problem. One enterprising butcher

In the cities, the blizzard halted food delivery, but many civic-minded businesses picked up the slack. Throughout the storm, Louis Fleischmann's Vienna Model Bakery in New York City stayed open all night and gave away baked goods to the hungry.

loaded a haunch of beef onto a cart he had fitted with runners and sold pieces of it to customers along the street, simply cutting what his customers wanted and charging what the market would allow. Although they may have grumbled about the rising prices, those with money paid the butchers for meat that would help keep up their strength in the cold.

Again, farmers and those living in small towns had fewer problems obtaining fresh meat during the storm. Of course, that didn't mean there weren't exceptions. Hartford, Connecticut, wasn't a large city, and sufficient food was probably available. But for at least one family that was irrelevant. The family, along with a dozen strangers who had taken refuge in their house early in the storm, awoke after a night's sleep to find themselves trapped inside. The huge snowfall had completely encased the house, sealing in not just the people but also hundreds of sparrows that had taken refuge under the back porch. With so many extra mouths to feed, the family quickly ran through its food supply. Finally, as stomachs rumbled, the family trapped sparrows and turned them into a tasty sparrow pie, allowing everyone to wait out the four days it took before neighbors arrived to dig them out.

Just as the poorer classes worried about the cold in their apartments, they also suffered from a lack of money to buy food. Meat was often too expensive for them in the best of times. During the storm it was well beyond their reach. Adults could stand hunger pains better than children. And babies couldn't last long at all without food. Milk, then, was a precious commodity for many families.

In New York City alone, 600,000 to 700,000 quarts of milk were normally consumed each day. When the blizzard struck, not a drop of fresh milk arrived in the city between Monday and Wednesday. To make matters

Using ropes to avoid losing his way, a man carries a child in the driving snow. The need to get food, particularly milk for babies, forced many people to risk life and limb in the severe blizzard conditions.

worse, no one kept a supply of milk at home because with daily delivery there was no need. This was true of both the wealthy and the poor, for both relied on the daily delivery service. Wealthy and middle-class residents counted on the milk cart to bring fresh milk from the country to the kitchen entrance of their townhouses. Residents of the tenements received a somewhat different, and cheaper, product. Unable to afford the farm-fresh produce, they relied on milk from cows that lived in the city in dirty, sunless barns. This milk was often diluted with water, then chalk was added as a whitener to disguise the trick. The result was a thin blue mixture. However, even thin blue milk was better than no milk, and residents of the tenement apartments welcomed the thin mixture poured into the pails they left on their doorsteps.

When the milk trains couldn't deliver, the shortage rapidly affected everyone in the city. For a few hours the supply of condensed milk on grocers' shelves helped, but that was quickly depleted. Then the price of milk soared. Normally 2¢ or 3¢ a quart, the price jumped to 10¢ or 15¢. Soon no amount of money could buy milk, and even the wealthy made their way to the train stations in a desperate search for milk for their children.

The New York Infant Asylum in Westchester County was home to 400 abandoned or orphaned children between the ages of two weeks and six years. Normally supplied with eight cans of milk a day by a dairy located eight miles away, the Infant Asylum was isolated by the storm for over a week. Disaster was averted only through the luck of a purchasing clerk's error. Just a few days before the storm, a supply of Borden canned condensed milk arrived. Instead of 12 dozen cans, 12 gross (1,728 cans) were delivered. The resident physician, Dr. Charles Gilmore Kerley, was afraid that condensed milk would make the infants sick, so he ordered it to be diluted with barley water. The result was a success. In fact, infants who had been difficult to feed began to gain weight. As a result of his experience during the blizzard, Dr. Kerley spent the next 50 years advocating the use of condensed milk for infant feeding.

In the countryside a different milk problem existed. There the supply was more than adequate, but distribution was impossible. Most farmers made it to their barns for the twice-daily milking, but the milk had nowhere to go. George Deuell's son watched his father frantically try to store the rapidly accumulating milk. The storm showed no sign of clearing and the cows continued to produce. George noted that his father would gladly have fed the milk back to the cows had they been willing to drink it. As the farmer's pails filled and he ran out of room to store his supply, his wife did what she could to help: she churned the milk into butter for safekeeping. Where farmers had plenty of pails to store the milk, Mother Nature's refrigeration system allowed them to keep their product until the storm cleared and they could find a market for it.

Despite the shortages of coal and food in the cities, there was no looting. Arrests for stealing groceries and other necessities were also fewer than usual in urban areas. A driver whose coal cart broke in front of a tenement building filled with cold families thought he would be overrun with thieves taking his precious cargo. Instead, more than 100 women and girls with pails and baskets appeared from the building and bought it all.

Despite the difficulties associated with feeding and warming themselves, some people in search of work found the blizzard a boon. This was especially true for young boys and immigrants. One particularly enterprising young man was Milton Daub, a 12-year-old living on East 145th Street in the South Bronx. Milton's neighborhood was a pleasant place filled with farms, estates, and small houses set well back from the street, with gardens in front of them.

When the storm struck, Milton and his three siblings quickly understood that school was canceled. Just as quickly, however, Milton's mother realized that although they had enough food for a day or two, they needed milk for the youngest children. Milton volunteered to go to the store, eventually convincing his parents that he knew what to do in a snowstorm. Part of the boy's argument

BLIZZARD HUMOR

Despite the problems the blizzard created, people still found time for a good laugh. A florist filled the snowdrift in front of his shop with unsold flowers, creating a bizarre wintry garden. On a roof-high drift a paint salesman wrote, "Now Is The Time To Paint Your Roof."

Wordplay was popular in the 19th century, and during the blizzard opportunities abounded to strike a humorous note with the words *snow, bank,* and *drift.* In the words of the wits of the day: Do you get my drift?

In another attempt at humor someone posted a sign in the snow that read in large letters: "500 Girls Wanted!" Young ladies who rushed to look at this promising opportunity then saw the small print: "to eat snow."

In what was perhaps not the kindest practical joke, two boys with energy to spare dug a 75-foot path through the snow. The unfortunate pedestrians who used the path eventually discovered that it stopped in a dead end.

A florist's attempt at brightening spirits through humor.

was that he had been studying Eskimos in school. Imitating the Eskimos and working with things he found in the house, Milton constructed snowshoes from wooden barrel hoops, wire, twine, pieces of canvas, and roller skates deprived of their wheels. Milton's father helped by constructing a wagon on runners by nailing a box top to a sledge. Since the front door was snowed in, Milton descended from the window with 50¢ in his pocket to buy milk.

Milton's snowshoes worked better than he could have expected: he was able to walk quickly down the street, pulling his sled. As he passed, neighbors called out requests for milk. When Milton reached the store, he bought 50¢ worth of condensed milk and started home. As he skimmed across the snow, he ran into many who were having difficulty reaching the store to buy desperately needed milk. Milton sold some of his and was rewarded with tips from thankful parents. In 20 minutes the enterprising boy had two dollars, and he returned to the store to buy a case of condensed milk. Milton worked busily all morning delivering milk to families who couldn't leave their homes, stopping only when he heard the noon whistle.

When Milton finally went back home, his parents were initially angry. After all, he had been gone for hours and they had been worried. But when they saw his pocketful of change, plus the three cans of milk he had saved for them, their anger turned to praise. After a warm lunch Milton bundled up again, this time wearing three pairs of wool socks to keep the cold away. By three in the afternoon Milton had sold all of the milk in his neighborhood store and had found another store with some still in stock. People also gave him money for prescriptions and groceries, accompanied by generous tips for his services.

Sometime after five o'clock, Milton finally called it a

day and returned home with a loaf of bread for his family, proud to have paid for part of their supper. After a hot meal he slept 12 hours.

The next morning Milton's mother asked if he knew how much money he had made. He didn't, but he was sure it was more than the cost of the bread and the milk he had brought them. When his mother told him that he had made $67.65, Milton couldn't believe it. (Today that would be equivalent to nearly $1,000.) On Tuesday Milton shoveled snow after school. On Wednesday he paid for his entire family to take a sleigh ride to see the snowy city.

The snowstorm also meant that many men who had no work were suddenly in great demand as snow shovelers. When businesses realized they couldn't reopen without cleared streets, they willingly paid for the backbreaking labor. As a result hundreds, possibly even thousands, found well-paying work, if only for a few days.

Not surprisingly, Sergeant Long was first to arrive at the Signal Service on the Monday morning of the storm. However, he was not alone for long. In fact, all of the employees showed up that stormy morning. Later some speculated that their military backgrounds accounted for their strong sense of duty. Sergeant Long had left earlier than usual to make it to work by walking across the Brooklyn Bridge. Another member of the staff, who had been on a stalled suburban elevated train, crawled more than a mile on top of the line of stranded trains to reach a station.

Once in the office, the men realized that their problems weren't over. The anemometer (an instrument that measures wind velocity) had frozen stiff and wasn't registering any information. The anemometer data would be valuable for a thorough understanding of the storm. The instrument was located on the tower of the Equitable Assurance Building. It was attached to a sliding iron pipe and held by a screw on the top of the pole. The pole was four inches around and rose 25 feet above the tower—which itself was 172 feet above the street. The men realized that the only way to fix the anemometer was to climb the pole.

Years later Chief Elias Dunn wrote that the wind was gusting about 75 mph, driving snow and ice before it. The conditions were so bad that Dunn didn't feel he could require one of his employees to make the dangerous climb. Then Sergeant Long stepped forward and volunteered.

At first Dunn refused, saying that Long was too heavy. If the pole snapped under his weight, he would fall to a certain death. But Long persisted, adding that the climb would be at his own risk. No one knows why Long insisted on volunteering; while the anemometer information would be valuable, it was not a matter of life or death.

Later, when he described the day's events, Chief Dunn observed that Sergeant Long climbed the slim pole without any support. When he reached the top, he adjusted the instrument and replaced some wiring with one hand, holding on to the pole with the other while the storm whipped at him. The wind pressure was so great, Dunn said, that it was difficult to stand up even when holding on to something, and it was impossible to inhale and exhale properly if facing the wind. Despite these conditions, Long worked until the instrument was repaired, preserving the principal records of the storm for later researchers.

The problems didn't end after the snow had stopped falling. For weeks city streets remained clogged with huge snowdrifts, in addition to downed utility poles and wires.

Cleaning Up

When temperatures rose above freezing on Wednesday, March 14, the storm was officially over. In the absence of strong winds and low temperatures, people were finally able to go outside and assess the damage. In some cases this meant discovering that their neighbors were snowed in. Neighborhood shoveling teams were not an uncommon sight as everyone worked together to free the trapped.

While freeing people from their homes was a relatively speedy process, complete recovery from a storm as powerful as the Blizzard of '88 was slow. Roof and window repair occupied many home and business owners. Elevated trains and railroad cars were uncovered and, if necessary, hauled back onto the tracks. Across cities and the countryside, downed electric, telephone, and cable lines had to be repaired. The delivery of food and coal had to be resumed. And before this could happen, mounds of snow had to be cleared.

A single snowflake feels weightless, but a shovelful of snow is heavy. Those who had shoveled snow at the height of the storm already knew how hard the job was. After the storm, even as temperatures rose, more snow had to be removed before businesses could open and residents could move freely along the streets. In New York City, Mayor Abram Stevens Hewitt assigned responsibility for the removal of snow to the superintendent of streets and roads. He also made the decision to allow snow to be dumped from any pier along the river, instead of the few normally reserved for dumping. Still, local merchants worried that the city lacked an organized snow-removal plan and wouldn't complete the job for weeks. So the merchants volunteered to clear the snow from the major city streets themselves. After receiving approval from the superintendent of streets and roads, the merchants gave priority to the main thoroughfares, which in addition to snow were clogged with fallen utility poles and wires.

In the days after the blizzard the worried businessmen were proved correct. The "Army of the Shovel" organized by the superintendent of streets and roads did not move as quickly as planned. Though the south sides of streets had been cleared, the north sides, piled high with drifts, remained clogged. When traffic moving in opposite directions met, horrible jams resulted, and inevitably someone's cart or horse got stuck in the snow again.

Throughout the affected states, property owners tunneled into huge drifts and lit fires in them. Unfortunately, the rapid runoff of melted snow caused serious flooding of gutters and basements in towns, and of cellars, barns, and fields in the country.

Most cities in the next century would link the duties

of garbage collection with those of snow removal. This would allow garbage collection routes to be followed when snow was cleared. Nineteenth-century cities lacked both systems. Garbage collection was poorly organized, and many households paid a man with a dogcart to take their trash away. The blizzard proved too much for the small dog-pulled carts; during the storm people were forced to burn their garbage in the kitchen stove. This utter breakdown of city sanitation caused by the storm was the trigger for a complete overhaul. Within a few years New York and other cities had established a permanent force to sweep and clean the streets daily. New ordinances forbade coal bins, sheds, and other obstacles on the sidewalks. In New York City the street cleaners wore white uniforms and once a year put on a parade down Fifth Avenue, marching with their brooms held like muskets over their shoulders.

In addition to armies of shoveling men, great wooden wheels were rolled down streets in some towns. The weight of the wheels pressed the snow flat, creating a hard path and clearing the way for traffic. In New Jersey a breeder of Saint Bernards put 10 of his dogs to work running back and forth to break a road to the railroad station. Given the large paws and thick fur of the dogs—a breed that originated in the mountains of Switzerland—these were probably the happiest participants in the snow-removal process.

Train lines slowly cleared. Chauncey Depew had been at his desk in New York City's Grand Central Station every day during the storm, and late on Wednesday he finally managed a tired smile. A train that left Albany that morning had arrived. Although the train was five hours late, its arrival meant that the line was clear. All along the railway lines, crews were digging the trains out of drifts. One 18-year-old passenger, tired of the inactivity on his stranded train, volunteered to join the work crew. Several weeks later he received a check for 60¢ from the railroad company, his wages for several hours' labor. Elsewhere there was simply too much snow to pretend the trains would move anytime soon. Passengers on these trains were evacuated by sleigh to other stations, where they could continue their journey on cleared tracks.

Delivery of food, especially milk, accompanied the clearing of snow. J. S. Alley and 100 of his neighbors broke a snowbound road and delivered 1,000 quarts of milk to New Haven on Wednesday. In Philadelphia man proved stronger than beast. A gang of shovelers was required to break the snow before a snowplow drawn by 28 horses could move through the drifts.

Some people were more lighthearted in their efforts to deal with the snow. A stranded honeymooning couple enjoyed the isolation of a town encased in snow. When the new husband went to the grocery store for supplies, he found a surprise for his bride. Back at the hotel he bundled her up and coaxed her outdoors, then set off the boxes and boxes of fireworks he had purchased, lighting up the sky for miles around. In New Haven one man hitched his flat-bottomed rowboat to his horse. He glided smoothly over drifts and ice, calmly seated in the stern of his new snowboat.

No matter the circumstances, the Blizzard of '88 made a lasting impression on those who lived through it. For decades newspapers marked the anniversary of the storm with special articles, and every snowstorm that followed was compared to the 1888 blizzard. Alfred E. Smith had watched people cross the East River from the window of his mother's home near the Brooklyn Bridge. Years later, in 1929, the memory of the storm was so strong that Al joined 14 other men in forming the Society of Blizzard Men in his hometown of New York City.

These 14 men first met to exchange reminiscences of their experiences during the three fateful days in March 1888. Their first meeting was so successful that by the following year they had more than 100 dues-paying members. Later expanded by the addition of Blizzard Ladies, the society met annually for a luncheon where memories of the storm could be exchanged. Perhaps, as Senator Conkling told the newspapers after the storm, if you hadn't seen it for yourself, tales of the blizzard sounded like products of an overactive imagination.

Beyond the individual memories, the effect upon city life was also strong. Mayor Hewitt had campaigned on promises of reform and improvement in New York City, and the blizzard was a big help to his efforts. Only a month before the storm, the state legislature had turned down his request for money for an underground subway. When the storm struck, the benefits of an underground transportation system became clearer. The prestigious *New York Times* commented, "An underground rapid transit system would have done what the elevated trains could not do. If the telegraph wires had been placed underground as contemplated by the law, they would have been made to subserve a specially important duty at a time when they were most sorely needed. . . . Stilled railway and telegraphic communication will no longer answer for this great city." The *Times* added that the storm "demonstrated the inadequacy of the elevated railroad system to such an emergency. . . . [It is] intolerable that the internal transit of New York City should be at the mercy of the elements. The ordinary business of the elevated roads [has] far outgrown their capacity, while they cannot even pretend to cope with great emergencies."

By March 18 the *Times* had published its own plan for a subway system. This proposal called for a line from the Battery at the southern tip of Manhattan all the way to

In the late 1880s a tangle of overhead telegraph and telephone wires was a common part of the urban landscape. The Blizzard of '88 provided the impetus for cities to require that utility lines be placed underground.

the north end of the island. The newspaper claimed that the plan would lead to other neighborhood improvements because of the increased ease of activity. Within 15 years a plan very much like this one was in place.

As serious as the transportation situation was the problem of overhead electric, telephone, and cable lines. Each utility company had its own poles. In New York City that included five different electric companies— each with poles 5 to nearly 10 stories tall. A single pole could carry between 100 and 200 wires, and with so many poles placed together there were thousands of wires running in all directions along the streets. In some places the wires were so thick that they blocked the view of the street from windows. The problem of electric poles had been acknowledged before the Blizzard of '88. Firemen found the thick web a hindrance to fire fighting, and in 1886 a law had been passed requiring all wires to be buried underground. No one enforced the law, however, and nothing had changed despite the best efforts of Mayor Hewitt.

When Hewitt was succeeded as mayor on January 1, 1889, the new mayor, Hugh Grant, made removal of the wires his top priority. He declared that the electric companies had 90 days to move their wires underground and that all new wires would also be underground. "When we fix a time we mean it," declared Grant. "When the time is ended the poles will come down." True to his word, Mayor Grant ordered the poles chopped down at the end of 90 days. Several companies had not complied. Millionaire Jay Gould, an owner of Western Union, complained that the removal of the poles was unconstitutional and obtained a court order to stop it. Within two weeks, however, the courts allowed the city to go ahead with the plan to remove utility poles. In mid-April the tall poles began to fall across Manhattan, and wires were rolled up and taken away. Although the electric companies had initially complained about the expense of maintaining and repairing underground lines, in the end the cost was lower.

The storm did much to temper American citizens' confidence in the progress of technology. The general feeling of the public was well captured by the *Hartford Courant,* which lampooned those who clung to the notion of a progressive 19th century in which beef could be

Horse-drawn wagons line up to dump snow in the river, New York. The blizzard prompted cities not only to assume responsibility for snow removal but also to create municipal garbage-collection services, a major advance in sanitation.

obtained from Chicago in two days, and milk delivered to one's door was cheaper than keeping a cow. Where was the benefit of that kind of progress if a storm meant no railroad, no telegraph, no horsecar, no milk, no delivery of food at the door? The *Courant* was afraid that the advantages of the century had turned back on the people.

But, spurred by failures during the blizzard, society would adapt. With underground transportation to guarantee workers a warm, rapid ride through stormy weather, and with the danger of fallen electric poles removed, most people agreed that the city was finally keeping up with the demands of the times.

Many members of the Blizzard Men and Ladies remembered the storm as a great communal adventure.

One noted, "It had its tragic side but curiously left in its wake mainly good will, and to its survivors it has become almost a household symbol standing not only for the storm itself but for all that was best in the 'good old days.'"

While this is true of the spirit that guided the cleanup and recovery, the blizzard was definitely a turning point for the city. Technology was no longer simply embraced; it was integrated into the fabric of the city. Similarly, growing cities realized that they had an obligation to their citizens to organize sanitation and utilities. The changes did not happen overnight, but the acknowledgment that they had to happen nearly did in the days between March 11 and March 13, 1888.

Chronology

1888   *March 10:* Northeastern United States enjoys a beautiful springlike Saturday; U.S. Signal Service forecasts continued "fair weather throughout the Atlantic States"

       March 11: Low-pressure system moves up east coast; by midnight the front has begun dumping rain, sleet, and snow from Washington, D.C., to the New England states

       March 12: By dawn 10 inches of snow have accumulated in New York City and other areas (by the end of the blizzard, some places will have received 50 inches); temperatures dip near zero, with wind gusts up to 84 mph; huge snowdrifts form; public transportation systems in cities are paralyzed; telegraph and telephone lines are down all over the Northeast; freight and passenger trains become stuck in the snow; winds blow much of the water out of the Potomac River near Washington and the Delaware River between Philadelphia and Camden, New Jersey, stranding ferries; at Lewes, Delaware, ships in harbor sink or are grounded, a tug crashes through a pier, and 11 men are stranded on the remnants of that pier for many hours; 14 schooners and several steam freighters run aground between Lewes and Cape Henlopen; a number of pilot boats sailing out of New York Harbor are caught in the storm, and nine pilot boats and a yacht on its maiden voyage are lost

       March 13: Storm begins to let up; a patchwork of ice floes stretching from Brooklyn to Manhattan clogs the East River; people attempting to cross the river are trapped when the tide turns and the ice floes break apart and begin drifting out to sea; brothers Gurton and Legrand Chappelle, ages nine and four, are rescued after spending 22 hours in a snow cave against a stone wall near Montville, Connecticut

       March 14: Temperatures rise above freezing, marking the official end of the blizzard; all told, the storm killed nearly 400 persons

       April 18: Former senator Roscoe Conkling, considered the final casualty of the blizzard, dies from complications of pneumonia

1929   Society of Blizzard Men (later to become Society of Blizzard Men and Ladies) is founded

Further Reading

Cable, Mary. *The Blizzard of '88.* New York: Atheneum, 1988.

Caplovich, Judd. *Blizzard! The Great Storm of '88.* Vernon, Conn.: Vero Publishing Co., 1987.

Goldstein, Mel. *The Complete Idiot's Guide to Weather.* New York: Alpha Books, 1999.

Hardy, Ralph. *Teach Yourself Weather.* Chicago: Teach Yourself Books, 1997.

Murphree, Tom, and Mary K. Miller. *Watching Weather, An Exploration Book.* New York: Henry Holt and Co., 1998.

Weather. Pleasantville, N.Y.: Readers Digest Association Inc., 1997.

Index

Index

Picture Credits

TRACEE DE HAHN is a freelance writer living in Lexington, Kentucky. In addition to her professional degree in architecture, she holds a master's degree in European history.

JILL McCAFFREY has served for four years as national chairman of the Armed Forces Emergency Services of the American Red Cross. Ms. McCaffrey also serves on the board of directors for Knollwood—the Army Distaff Hall. The former Jill Ann Faulkner, a Massachusetts native, is the wife of Barry R. McCaffrey, a member of President Bill Clinton's cabinet and director of the White House Office of National Drug Control Policy. The McCaffreys are the parents of three grown children: Sean, a major in the U.S. Army; Tara, an intensive care nurse and captain in the National Guard; and Amy, a seventh grade teacher. The McCaffreys also have two grandchildren, Michael and Jack.